Esther

Becoming a Girl of Purpose

DANNAH GRESH

with Sarah Giordano

MOODY PUBLISHERS

CHICAGO

© 2024 by
DANNAH GRESH

Unless otherwise indicated, all Scripture quotations are taken from the *Holy Bible*, New Living Translation, copyright © 1996, 2004, 2015 by Tyndale House Foundation. Used by permission of Tyndale House Publishers, Carol Stream, Illinois 60188. All rights reserved.

Scripture quotations marked MSG are taken from *The Message,* copyright © 1993, 2002, 2018 by Eugene H. Peterson. Used by permission of NavPress. All rights reserved. Represented by Tyndale House Publishers.

Scripture quotations marked (NIV) are taken from the Holy Bible, New International Version®, NIV®. Copyright © 1973, 1978, 1984, 2011 by Biblica, Inc.™ Used by permission of Zondervan. All rights reserved worldwide. www.zondervan.com The "NIV" and "New International Version" are trademarks registered in the United States Patent and Trademark Office by Biblica, Inc.™

All emphasis in Scripture has been added.

Edited by Ashleigh Slater
Interior and cover design: Julia Ryan
Cover and interior illustrations: Julia Ryan
Interior illustration of pink flower copyright © 2023 by windesign/Shutterstock (28909644). All rights reserved.
Interior illustration of magnifying glass copyright © 2023 by M. Stasy/Shutterstock (115513243). All rights reserved.
Interior illustration of treasure chest copyright © 2023 by Pagina/Shutterstock (106348796). All rights reserved.
Interior illustration of autumn leaves copyright © 2023 by Green Flame/Shutterstock (1493892203). All rights reserved.
Interior illustration of dice copyright © 2023 by yusufdemirci/Shutterstock (2310155685). All rights reserved.
Interior illustration of star of David copyright © 2023 by Yulia Glam/Shutterstock (138182342). All rights reserved.
Interior illustration of Purim carnival copyright © 2023 by girafchik/Shutterstock (2117190260). All rights reserved.
Interior illustration of hamantaschen cookies copyright © 2023 by Oksana Mizina/Shutterstock (1871058547). All rights reserved.
Interior illustration of baking elements copyright © 2023 by Tetyana Snezhyk/Shutterstock (247388569). All rights reserved.
Interior illustration of Islamic design elements copyright © 2023 by Ardea-studio/Shutterstock (2115183614). All rights reserved.
Interior illustration of Indian elephant copyright © 2023 by Reinekke/Shutterstock (1217201086). All rights reserved.
Interior illustration of boxer gloves copyright © 2023 by Oleon17/Shutterstock (1570826344). All rights reserved.
Interior illustration of Egyptian scroll copyright © 2023 by Oleksandra Klestova/Shutterstock (2128693343). All rights reserved.
Author photo: London Wolf

Printed by Versa Press in East Peoria, IL – May 2024

Library of Congress Cataloging-in-Publication Data

Names: Gresh, Dannah, 1967- author. | Giordano, Sarah, author.
Title: Esther : becoming a girl of purpose / Dannah Gresh with Sarah
  Giordano.
Description: Chicago : Moody Publishers, [2024] | Series: True girl Bible
  study | Includes bibliographical references. | Audience: Ages 8-12 |
  Summary: "Esther was given one of the world's hardest assignments: to
  protect God's special people from an evil plan. But it wasn't because
  she was extra-brave or super-extraordinary. Her life reminds us that
  every True Girl has a purpose and that it sometimes takes great patience
  to live it out"-- Provided by publisher.
Identifiers: LCCN 2023057939 (print) | LCCN 2023057940 (ebook) | ISBN
  9780802422439 (paperback) | ISBN 9780802499394 (ebook)
Subjects: LCSH: Esther, Queen of Persia--Juvenile literature. | Esther,
  Queen of Persia--Textbooks. | Girls--Religious life--Juvenile
  literature. | BISAC: JUVENILE NONFICTION / Religious / Christian /
  Inspirational | JUVENILE NONFICTION / Girls & Women
Classification: LCC BS580.E8 G74 2024 (print) | LCC BS580.E8 (ebook) |
  DDC 222/.9--dc23/eng/20240422
LC record available at https://lccn.loc.gov/2023057939
LC ebook record available at https://lccn.loc.gov/2023057940

Originally delivered by fleets of horse-drawn wagons, the affordable paperbacks from D. L. Moody's publishing house resourced the church and served everyday people. Now, after more than 125 years of publishing and ministry, Moody Publishers' mission remains the same—even if our delivery systems have changed a bit. For more information on other books (and resources) created from a biblical perspective, go to: www.moodypublishers.com or write to:

Moody Publishers
820 N. LaSalle Boulevard
Chicago, IL 60610

1 3 5 7 9 10 8 6 4 2

Printed in the United States of America

Table of Contents

My Notes on Esther

As you study the life of Esther, you can come back to this page to write down important thoughts and observations about her and the most important people in her story. Turn here anytime you learn something you don't want to forget or when I remind you.

_____   _____   _____   _____

{ Her Uncle }   { The Queen }   { The King }   { The Bad Guy }

THE PERSIAN EMPIRE

My Map of Esther's World

Esther lived in Susa but she didn't call it "home." As we study her life, you're going to come back to this map to complete mini-assignments with big impact and record Esther's lessons on purpose.

GREECE
ATHENS

AEGEAN SEA

SARDIS

ANCYRA

BLACK SEA

TARSUS

MEDITERRANEAN SEA

CYRENE
LIBYA

DAMASC

MEMPHIS

EGYPT

THEBES

RED SEA

ARAL
SEA

CASPIAN SEA

MARACANDA

BACTRA

TAXILA

ARBELA

ECBATANA

PERSIA

BABYLON

ASPANDA

SUSA

PASARGADAE

INDIA

PERSEPOLIS

PERSIAN
GULF

ARABIAN SEA

PURPOSE LESSONS

We're going to study the life of Esther to learn six important lessons about **purpose**. Sometimes I will invite you to come back to this page and write down what you're learning!

PURPOSE LESSON #2

PURPOSE LESSON #1

PURPOSE LESSON #6

Purpose

········► **Fill in the blanks!**

Purpose: the _____ something _____ .

PURPOSE LESSON #3

PURPOSE LESSON #4

PURPOSE LESSON #5

How to Study the Bible
(Zooming, Zeroing & Zipping Basics!)

If you've never done a True Girl Bible study, this explanation
of our Bible study method is really important. Make sure you
read it so that you get the most out of your time in God's Word!

If you've done a True Girl Bible study before,
you can skip this and go straight to chapter 1.

I'm so happy you've decided to dig into this Bible study to learn about the life and purpose of Esther! If you're here, you've surely heard of something called the Bible. After all, it is the bestselling book in all of history. But, have you ever stopped and wondered: *Why is this book so special?* Well, my friend, that's a very good question, and I'm so glad you asked!

What is the Bible, Really?

The Bible contains the story of God's relationship with His creation. Although it's all bound together into one book, the Bible is actually a collection of a bunch of different books written by forty writers. These books contain stories, poems, songs, prayers, and more. Some of these people wrote about their experiences with God, and some wrote about how they saw God's story playing out in front of them. Every word of the Bible is *inspired by God*, which means that God was leading the authors and telling them exactly what to write! That means the Bible is God's Word, so it's the ultimate source of truth! (After all, who knows it better than God?)

All Scripture is inspired by God and is useful to teach us what is true and to make us realize what is wrong in our lives. It corrects us when we are wrong and teaches us to do what is right. (2 Timothy 3:16)

Fast-forward to today, and guess what? The authors who wrote down the Bible may not be around anymore, but the Bible certainly is. God's story (and purpose) isn't complete yet and is continuing with you!

So, as we participate in the story of God's relationship with His creation, we look to the Bible to find the truth of who God is and who we are meant to be. (This helps us understand how we fit into God's purpose.) We can use the Bible to learn what is right and wrong. It teaches us how to walk through life, and how to survive in hard times. It helps us know how to express gladness in good times. And best of all, it trains us how to have a relationship with the God who loves us so much!

Your word is a lamp to guide my feet and a light for my path. (Psalm 119:105)

Why do the stories in the Bible matter to you?

As you read through the Bible's stories, you might think, *What does this have to do with me?* The people in the Bible lived a long time ago, probably far across the world from where you live now, and had a totally different way of living. At first look, it may seem like you have nothing in common with the people and places you read about, but don't give up so quickly! Keep looking. These are stories about real, ordinary people in history who experienced God! The same God who loves you and me today. We study the Bible to learn more about our loving God and how we can better live to honor Him.

Since the Bible is the Word of God, it is full of truth. But sometimes, the truth is buried below surface level, making it a bit tricky to understand. In this Bible study, we are going to roll up our sleeves to study the Bible and uncover amazing truth-treasures!

Have you ever found a buried treasure?

Imagine this: You've embarked on a hike through some woods near your neighborhood. You're stepping on the dried autumn leaves, and you hear *crunch, crackle, crackle, crunch!* But suddenly, you step and hear something more like a *crunch, crackle, thump!* You kick the leaves away and look below to discover that your trail has been interrupted by something smooth and solid. As you glance down, you realize you're standing on what looks to be the lid of a great big wooden chest! You get on your hands and knees and begin digging it out with your bare hands. It takes all your strength to lift it up, but wow, this chest looks olllld! You pry its creaky lid open and the sun's light floods inside for the first time in who knows how long. The stale smell of mildew rises from within the box as your eyes fall upon a note! The fragile letter is dated 50 years ago and was written by a girl who lived in the same neighborhood you live in. It's all about what life was like in your neighborhood those 50 years ago! She writes about who lived in the neighborhood, their plans for the annual Fourth of July cookout, and then the best part—she writes about a hidden hiking trail. Apparently, it leads to the best views in all of the forest!

You just uncovered a really cool look into the history of your neighborhood! Of course, you decide to find that hiking trail right away and follow it up to the highest point in the woods. Your legs are sore, but you keep climbing, and after a couple of forks in the road and lots of sweat, you discover a beautiful view of your neighborhood that you've never seen before!

The Bible is kind of like that letter. Yes, it's very old (thousands of years old, in fact!), but it's a wayyyy better treasure! It tells us the story of how God loves His people in this world and even helps us see things differently if we follow the trails of those who've lived and walked before us. There is so much we can learn from it and apply to our own lives.

How do we study the Bible?

At True Girl, we have developed a really cool way to study the Bible. We call it the **Four-Z Method of Bible Study**! All you have to do is:

ZOOM **ZOOM** ZERO **ZIP**!

We will teach you how to:

⭐ **ZOOM IN**—understand the details
⭐ **ZOOM OUT**—get the big picture
⭐ **ZERO IN**—find out what it really means
⭐ **ZIP IT UP**—learn what God wants you to do with it

Whew, that was fast! Let me explain it a bit more slowly.

The basics of Zooming— Who? What? Where? When? Why?

We'll be doing a lot of **ZOOMING**! That's when we understand the *who*, *what*, *when*, *where*, and *why*! Zooming is the most time-consuming part of Bible study. As you observe, you ask and answer a lot of questions. As we examine the life of Esther, I'll ask the questions and you get to answer them. (We'll make this fun with quizzes, puzzles, and cool clues.) Sometimes we'll clearly be zooming out. And other times we'll clearly be zooming in. But sometimes it's a big mixture of both at the same time.

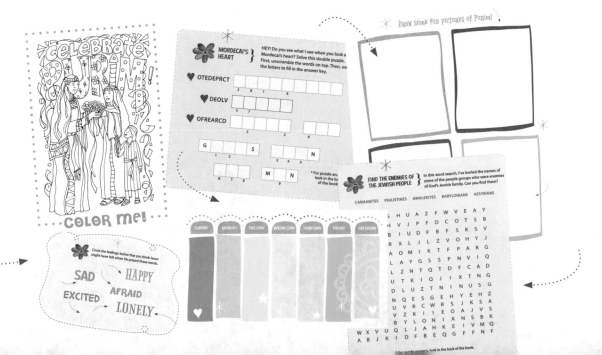

ZOOM OUT!

One way to get a better understanding of what the Bible means is to look at the *context*.

·······▶ { **context:** the background of the story }

To see the context, we "zoom out" and look for what else was going on in the background. Our goal is to better understand the time, place, and people. It's kind of like hiking up that secret path to get a bird's-eye view of your neighborhood. We ask questions like:

- ★ **When** did this happen?
- ★ **Where** did it happen?
- ★ **Who** was there?

- ★ **What** else was happening at that time?
- ★ **Why** did God allow it in their lives?

The answers help us understand the story.

ZOOM IN!

Another way to gain a better understanding of what something in the Bible means for us is to look at the *particulars*.

·······▶ { **particulars:** the details of the story }

To see the particulars, we dig deeper below the surface—like when you step on a treasure chest and lean down to uncover and lift it up! These details are more clearly seen when we *zoom in* on a word or a phrase to figure out what it really means.

This gets a little tricky when we're studying the Bible. Why? Well, did you know that the Bible wasn't originally written in English? The Bible has two parts—the Old Testament and the New Testament. Esther's story comes from the Old Testament, which was written in the Hebrew language with the exception of a few parts.

·······▶ { **Hebrew:** the original language the Old Testament was written in }

In Hebrew, some words mean something different than they do in English. For example, say I shout, "Heads up!" You probably know that means to "duck" and you would put your head down (not up). Well, if you translate that directly into another language, someone might actually lift their head high into the air. (And they might get hit with a baseball or something!)

Unless you understand ancient Hebrew, you won't understand everything you study about Esther.

Let me give you an example. The book of Esther ends with a Jewish feast called *Purim.* You might think, *What a nice name for a holiday!* But when we zoom in on the word *Purim* to understand the particulars, we get a really powerful look at what's happening in the story.

You see, there is a bad guy in this story who liked to roll dice. Yes, like the kind you use to play Monopoly. Only in the book of Esther, the stakes are much higher than buying the properties of Boardwalk and Park Place. The dice were thrown to pick a date for Esther's death.

Here's where zooming in gets interesting!

You see, in ancient Hebrew, the word for "dice" is *pur.* I don't want to get too far ahead of ourselves, but Esther ends up using that word to throw a real big celebration. In fact, it's a party so big it's still celebrated today.

The word *pur* was meant for Esther's destruction, but it became a word to mark her victory!

As we study Esther, be prepared to zoom in on the particulars—including specific words—because we'll get a much clearer understanding of what's happening in her story.

ZERO IN: What does it mean?

Once we've considered the *context* (by zooming out) and the *particulars* (by zooming in), we'll need to think a little harder to uncover *why* this story or truth is in the Bible. You're going to have the opportunity to ZERO IN, or focus, on what it might mean *for you*! Once again, I've got ya, True Girl! I'm going to help you do this with questions, and you'll get to fill in the answers.

ZIP IT UP: What does God want me to do with it?

To complete your study, you'll need to respond to God. After all, the Bible contains His words . . . so when you read it . . . well, if you don't respond, that's kinda just like a one-sided conversation. During this study, you'll have the opportunity to obey, agree with, or even question God. (Sometimes it can feel wrong to question Him, but I promise that it's OK to ask God questions. He wants you to express your thoughts and feelings to Him.) At the end of every chapter, you'll wrap up by talking to God about what you've learned. Then you can ask Him what to do with what you've discovered. You'll get to **ZIP IT UP** with God!

Welcome to the True Girl 4-Z Method of Bible Study!

All of this zooming, zipping, and zeroing is really a fun way to enter into what's called the Inductive Method of Bible Study. Some people use big, boring words to learn how to study the Bible, but I think it should be fun. So, my team and I reworked it and named it the **4-Z Method of Bible Study**.

What you'll Need

- ⭐ Your Bible (You won't use it a lot, but that's because I'm keeping this Bible study simple. All of the verses you'll need are printed right in this book. BUT, that's no excuse to not keep it with ya! I want you to get in the habit of having your very own treasured Bible on hand and marking it up as you study!)
- ⭐ This copy of *Esther: Becoming a Girl of Purpose*
- ⭐ Some colored markers or pencils

Got it all? OK. Let's get those creative juices flowin' by using the **4-Z Method** as we study the eventful life of an ordinary girl—Esther.

✳ What Is Purpose?

Imagine you are planting a garden. You have a lot of decisions to make! Maybe you will decide to plant lots of white and yellow daisies so you have something beautiful to look at every time you come home. Perhaps you will choose blossoms that attract butterflies so you can watch them fly by. Or maybe you will plant a garden full of yummy watermelons and cantaloupes so you have the most delicious summer ever. **Whatever you decide, it is clear that each type of plant has a purpose.**

So, let's talk about *purpose!* Do you have any idea what it means? Take a second to think about it, and then write your best guess below!

_____

_____

_____

OK, let's see if you're right!

What is PURPOSE?

As we study the life of Esther, we'll discover that she had a special purpose. And we'll learn that we do too. Here's a simple definition of the word:

········► { **PURPOSE: the reason something exists** }

Turn to page 11 and fill in the blanks to define the word *purpose.*

I have a patio garden at home! This year, I planted two cherry tomato plants. They have a purpose: to feed my twin granddaughters, Addie and Zoe, yummy cherry tomatoes. (Because they love tomatoes.)

Thankfully, my itty-bitty cherry tomato plants came with an instruction tag. So, I not only knew what their purpose was, but how to get the result I wanted. The instructions told me how much water and sunlight to give my plants. And they grew nice and tall and made lots of tomatoes.

What's YOUR purpose?

So, what's **YOUR** purpose? You didn't come with an instruction tag! But, if you are a Christian, the Bible can help. It is our instruction manual!

Use your favorite color pencil or pen to underline the two words—"plans" and "determines"—in the verse below.

 We can make our plans, but the LORD determines our steps.
(Proverbs 16:9)

We make many plans for our lives. Let's look a little closer, though.

Go back to the verse and circle the word **BUT!**

We make plans, **BUT GOD** *determines* our steps. He's ultimately working to guide us to be a part of His plan.

That simply means God has thought about you and how you fit into His big plan for the world. Your life is like a journey, and God is at work to guide you to take the right steps in the right direction. Why? So you can do what He has determined you should do.

This brings us to our very first lesson for this Bible study!

PURPOSE LESSON #1:
God has a plan for your life.

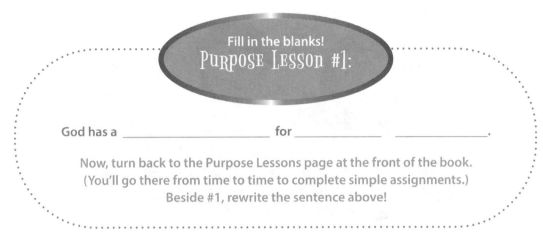

Fill in the blanks!
PURPOSE LESSON #1:

God has a _____ for _____ _____.

Now, turn back to the Purpose Lessons page at the front of the book.
(You'll go there from time to time to complete simple assignments.)
Beside #1, rewrite the sentence above!

The first thing you need to know about your purpose is you have one! And the Bible does contain a lot of things to help you know and understand what God *determines* for you to do with your life.

In this Bible study, we'll take a closer look at God's master plan and how you fit into it. Looks like we need to **start zooming!**

Zoom In & Out—Who? What? Where? When? Why?

ZOOM OUT!

To learn about *purpose*, we have to **ZOOM OUT** and look at why God made us to begin with. (That's a lot of zooming!) We're going waaaayyyyy back to the beginning. The book of Genesis tells us something important about why God created the first man and woman.

Read the verse below and underline the words that tell us who we resemble. (Hint: You'll find it mentioned two times!)

 So God created human beings in his own image.
In the image of God he created them;
male and female he created them. (Genesis 1:27)

You were created in God's "image" or likeness. That means you were created to make people remember and think about God, because there are things about you that are like Him. **How cool is that?**

When we read our user manual, it's not about us. It's all about Him. It might seem like we are reading about people like Ruth or Miriam or Esther. But when you really think about it, we are actually reading about all the ways God was working in their lives. Their lives point to Him. So do ours.

How do we use our lives to point to God? (Glad ya asked.)

Grab two pencils in different colors. Circle the two words in Genesis 1:27 that refer to the two different kind of people God created.

You probably circled the words *male* and *female*. These are two of the things that remind people about God. Of course, there are a lot of things about us that make us in God's image. Our brains. Our creativity. But God only mentions *male* and *female* in this verse. That means being a girl is a big deal. (So is being a boy. *We are both equally important!*)

But WHY did God create two different sexes, or genders?

It's because He wants us to look like Him. You might be wondering: *How does being a girl or a boy help us do* THAT?

Well, God is three different persons, who are really ONE. God the Father, God the Son, and God the Holy Spirit make up what's called the Trinity. ▶

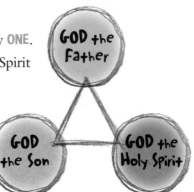

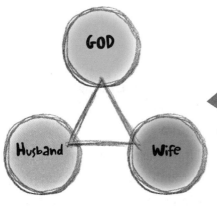

◀ When God created us as *male* and *female*, He gave us the ability to be two completely different people who could be joined together by marriage through God into ONE.

Does that mean you *have* to get married? No! But God created two genders. Male. Female. And it's important that you help to protect that Truth. Because God says it is a very important part of our ultimate purpose as humans: to help people remember and think about God.

But there's more! Let's keep reading from the first book of the Bible. What's the first thing God did after He created the first man and woman?

Double underline the first four words of this verse.

 Then God blessed them and said, "Be fruitful and multiply. Fill the earth and govern it. Reign over the fish in the sea, the birds in the sky, and all the animals that scurry along the ground." (Genesis 1:28)

God didn't just create men and women and leave them there in the garden like some statues of Himself. **He blessed them.** That means He declared them highly favored and special, unlike anything else He created.

You see, God created humans to be in a special loving relationship with Him. As a matter of fact, the whole Bible is a love story about God and how He interacts with us. And it is a user manual for how we can respond to His blessing and love and learn our purpose.

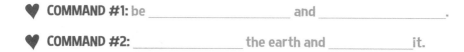

OK, let's look at Genesis 1:28 again for one more important piece of our purpose. Circle any commands or directions God gave to the first man and woman. (Hint: There are two but it might look like four!) When you find them, write them below:

♥ **COMMAND #1:** be _____ and _____.

♥ **COMMAND #2:** _____ the earth and _____ it.

God gave the first two humans the special task of making more humans. And to take care of the world. We're kind of like His representatives here on earth, caring for what He created and reminding everyone about Him because of our resemblance.

Maybe you're thinking, *What does this have to do with* MY *purpose?*

Well, when you understand God's plan for the world it will help you understand how you fit in. You see, our purpose is to let people see God through our lives. For example, when God told Moses to lead the Israelites out of slavery in Egypt, God used Moses to display His power. In that story, we see God part the Red Sea so the people could walk across on dry land. When the people were hungry, God caused manna (a food kind of like bread) to fall from the sky to provide for them. In every piece of Moses's life, we can see God. That's because Moses, God's blessed image bearer, was playing his part in making God famous.

ESTHER

OK, that was a super wide zoom. Let's start to look at how Esther fits into God's big plan.

Esther has a whole book of the Bible named after her. (Only one other woman has that honor: Ruth!)

Esther's life is an incredible story! We will see that she takes her assignment to govern or rule the earth seriously. She plays her important role in caring for God's world when she saves His special people, the Jews, from destruction. What Esther does causes all the Jewish people to throw a super big party to celebrate what God did.

But wait!

There's one thing you need to know about this book of the Bible: God is not mentioned even ONCE!

Wait a minute! *I thought it was all about HIM?* Well, remember when we said that all the stories of the Bible are really about all the ways God works through our lives? **AND** how God is made famous through our lives? Esther's story is a magnificent example of God's *providence*.

Providence is just a big word to describe the protective care of God. And it's happening all around us. All of the time! What is providence? One way to help you remember the meaning of providence is to break it down. Can you see another smaller word at the beginning of the word *providence*?

Write the shorter word here:

⟫⟶ _____

God provides. Even when we cannot see Him at work.

In your own words, write out a definition for *providence*.

⟫⟶ _____

_____

_____

_____

You've probably heard the word *providence* before. And you've probably experienced it.

Think about if you are hungry. Your mom or dad provides you with food! (But it's really God who made it grow.) When you grow out of your clothes, an older sibling might provide you with hand-me-downs. (Again, God made the cotton and sheep wool, right?)

Providence becomes really important when things aren't going so well. And that brings us back to our girl Esther.

Things were **NOT** going so great in Susa, where Esther lived. Let's begin our study of her life by meeting a guy named King Xerxes. It's time to **zoom in**.

ZOOM IN!

ESTHER 1:1-4

Read the Bible passage below. Use a purple pencil or marker to draw a squiggly line under every location you read about. Include cities, countries, and empires.

1 These events happened in the days of King Xerxes, who reigned over 127 provinces stretching from India to Ethiopia. *2* At that time Xerxes ruled his empire from his royal throne at the fortress of Susa. *3* In the third year of his reign, he gave a banquet for all his nobles and officials. He invited all the military officers of Persia and Media as well as the princes and nobles of the provinces. *4* The celebration lasted 180 days—a tremendous display of the opulent wealth of his empire and the pomp and splendor of his majesty.

These verses introduce King Xerxes who was the ruler of a **HUGE** kingdom!

If you didn't already underline "127 provinces," do it now! That's a lot of territory to rule.

Let's look at the map of the Persian Empire in the front of this book again. Circle the city of Susa. Then, use a purple pencil or pen to draw a boundary line or border around the area ruled by King Xerxes. It's all the land in the middle without all the diagonal lines through it.

Yep, King Xerxes ruled *a lot* of land and apparently it was totally going to his head. He believed it was all "his."

Look at Esther 1:1–4 again and circle every time the possessive pronoun "his" is used.

Each time the word "his" shows up in those verses, it's indicating King Xerxes possessed or owned something.

In the Bible passage, underline the things that he believed were his.

Do you see the same problem that I see? Remember when we said that our purpose is to make God famous? Well, I think our friend King Xerxes has some things a little bit confused. He thinks **he** is supposed to be the famous one! How famous? Well, he threw a party that lasted 180 days! That's **SIX MONTHS** of partying! What was the purpose of his party? To display all the things that were, in his mind, **HIS**.

THE PURPOSE OF THE PARTY }

The purpose of King Xerxes' party was to show off all the things that he thought were **HIS**. Find these four words that tell us what **HE** possessed.

WEALTH   POMP   SPLENDOR   MAJESTY

```
R  K  C  J  I  V  F  N  O  L
M  I  O  L  I  Q  U  O  W  F
A  D  U  P  W  E  A  L  T  H
J  F  J  O  C  E  W  C  X  L
E  L  Z  M  M  M  X  N  B  K
S  W  W  P  P  F  J  H  B  W
T  S  P  L  E  N  D  O  R  H
Y  F  N  U  R  C  R  I  Y  T
Y  W  X  X  F  T  H  C  X  M
N  E  D  J  A  M  F  K  T  W
```

* For puzzle answers, look in the back of the book.

I don't need a dictionary to know those words are pretty fancy schmancy! These are words that make King Xerxes famous. Not God.

I think there was a big problem in Susa, don't you?

Well, you'd think King Xerxes would have been pretty tired after six whole months of partying, but he was not done yet! Read on to find out what happens next. You'll soon see a total of *three* big problems in Susa. You've already discovered the first one:

➤ PROBLEM #1:
**King Xerxes thought life was all about him.
So, the wrong person was being made famous!**

When we attempt to make ourselves famous rather than God, we are working outside of our purpose. King Xerxes could have thrown a party to celebrate all the ways God had blessed him. But, instead, he made it all about HIM—his possessions, his position, and his power.

And . . . now . . . at the end of that looooong celebration, he decided he needed one more party! Well, it was called a banquet.

ESTHER 1:5-8

In the verses below, circle all of the possessions King Xerxes used at his banquet to remind people how wealthy he was.

5 When it was all over, the king gave a banquet for all the people, from the greatest to the least, who were in the fortress of Susa. It lasted for seven days and was held in the courtyard of the palace garden.

6 The courtyard was beautifully decorated with white cotton curtains and blue hangings, which were fastened with white linen cords and purple ribbons to silver rings embedded in marble pillars. Gold and silver couches stood on a mosaic pavement of porphyry, marble, mother-of-pearl, and other costly stones. 7 Drinks were served in gold goblets of many designs, and there was an abundance of royal wine, reflecting the king's generosity. 8 By edict of the king, no limits were placed on the drinking, for the king had instructed all his palace officials to serve each man as much as he wanted.

Have you ever been to a city? Maybe you live in one! Think of how many people are there. Can you imagine inviting EVERYONE IN THE CITY to a party at your house? Would they fit?

Well, that's exactly what King Xerxes did. He invited everyone in the city to the courtyard of the palace garden for seven days. The very fact that everyone fit into his palace was another way he boasted about his wealth! King Xerxes was putting HIS power and wealth on display.

Before we learn about problem number two, we need to meet another character in the story—Queen Vashti. King Xerxes' wife was putting on her own party for the women of the palace when the king called for her to come to his banquet. Did the queen follow the king's orders?

ESTHER 1:9-12

Underline Queen Vashti's decision.

9 At the same time, Queen Vashti gave a banquet for the women in the royal palace of King Xerxes. **10** On the seventh day of the feast, when King Xerxes was in high spirits because of the wine, he told the seven eunuchs who attended him—Mehuman, Biztha, Harbona, Bigtha, Abagtha, Zethar, and Carcas— **11** to bring Queen Vashti to him with the royal crown on her head. He wanted the nobles and all the other men to gaze on her beauty, for she was a very beautiful woman. **12** But when they conveyed the king's order to Queen Vashti, she refused to come. This made the king furious, and he burned with anger.

Turn back to the page at the front of the book labeled "My Notes On Esther." I think you're ready to write in some information about The King. Add his name and write down what you know about him.

Whoa! Queen Vashti refused a direct order from the king?! In Persia, that was a big no-no.

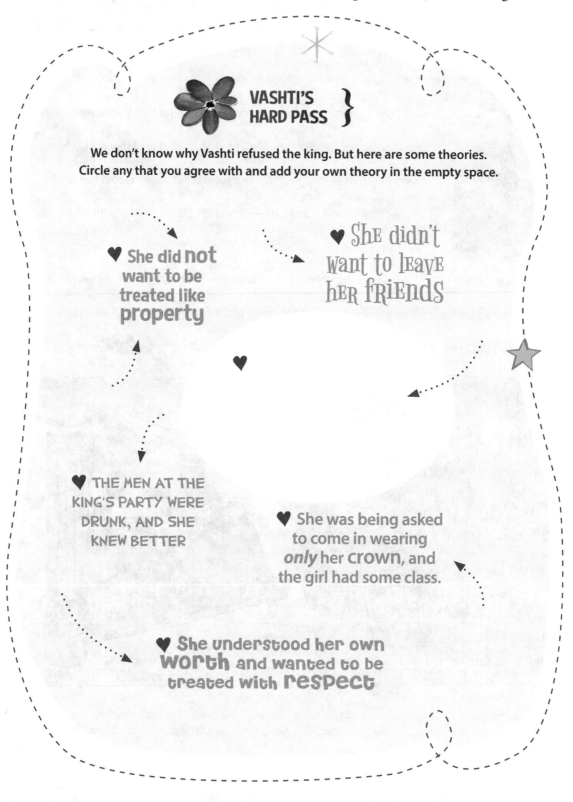

VASHTI'S HARD PASS }

We don't know why Vashti refused the king. But here are some theories. Circle any that you agree with and add your own theory in the empty space.

♥ She did **not** want to be treated like **property**

♥ SHE didn't want to leave HER fRiEnds

♥ THE MEN AT THE KING'S PARTY WERE DRUNK, AND SHE KNEW BETTER

♥ She was being asked to come in wearing *only* her **crown**, and the girl had some class.

♥ She understood her own **worth** and wanted to be treated with **respect**

We don't know why Queen Vashti said no. But it seemed to have something to do with understanding that the men in Susa did not understand the value of women. Of course, Queen Vashti's refusal made the king very mad.

And that brings us to . . .

PROBLEM #2:
King Xerxes got advice from people instead of God. Uh-oh!

King Xerxes is embarrassed by the queen's decision, but doesn't know what to do. So, he gets help.

ESTHER 1:13-22

Underline the names of who King Xerxes asks for advice. Put a square around the advice the king decides to follow.

13 He immediately consulted with his wise advisers, who knew all the Persian laws and customs, for he always asked their advice. 14 The names of these men were Carshena, Shethar, Admatha, Tarshish, Meres, Marsena, and Memucan—seven nobles of Persia and Media. They met with the king regularly and held the highest positions in the empire. 15 "What must be done to Queen Vashti?" the king demanded. "What penalty does the law provide for a queen who refuses to obey the king's orders, properly sent through his eunuchs?"* 16 Memucan answered the king and his nobles, "Queen Vashti has wronged not only the king but also every noble and citizen throughout your empire. 17 Women everywhere will begin to despise their husbands when they learn that Queen Vashti has refused to appear before the king. 18 Before this day is out, the wives of all the king's nobles throughout Persia and Media will hear what the queen did and will start treating their husbands the same way. There will be no end to their contempt and anger."

19 "So if it please the king, we suggest that you issue a written decree, a law of the Persians and

{ *What's a *eunuch*? For the purpose of our studies, what you need to know
  is that they were men who helped the kings and queens of Persia.

Medes that cannot be revoked. It should order that Queen Vashti be forever banished from the presence of King Xerxes, and that the king should choose another queen more worthy than she.

20 When this decree is published throughout the king's vast empire, husbands everywhere, whatever their rank, will receive proper respect from their wives!" 21 The king and his nobles thought this made good sense, so he followed Memucan's counsel. 22 He sent letters to all parts of the empire, to each province in its own script and language, proclaiming that every man should be the ruler of his own home and should say whatever he pleases.

Did you see "God" included in the list of those the king asked for advice in verses 13 and 14? Circle your answer.

Yep, he for sure prayed.

Nope, he forgot to ask the one who matters most!

I don't know about you, but that puts up a red flag for me. You see, when we ask for advice, it influences how we feel about our purpose. It doesn't change our purpose. God created us with a purpose that does not change: *to make Him famous*. But when we surround ourselves with people who are not seeking God, we forget our purpose and begin to make plans to make ourselves important.

And look at that, I think we've found another problem in our story!

▶ PROBLEM #3:
King Xerxes had the wrong user manual!

The Bible is the ultimate authority for our lives. That means that we can depend on it for Truth. It's our user manual. If someone says something or we read something and we're not sure if it's true, we can use the Bible to check!

On the other hand, what were King Xerxes' consultants turning to for their user manual? Let's look back at Esther 1:13. There are two things it says the counselors knew. What are those two things?

Fill in the blanks.

The king's wise advisers knew all the _____ and _____.

The king's counselors were using Persian laws and customs as their user manual! And that ended up with some pretty clear advice. Let's ZOOM IN on some of the things they were saying.

BOYS VS. GIRLS }
Using the hints after each sentence, fill in the blanks.

1 Memucan said that Queen Vashti had wronged the _____ and every _____ and _____ throughout the empire. (Hint: Read Esther 1:16.)

2 Then Memucan said that women everywhere will begin to _____ their husbands when they learn what Queen Vashti has done. (Hint: Read Esther 1:17.)

3 Memucan tells the king to issue a decree so that husbands everywhere will receive proper _____ from their wives. (Hint: Read Esther 1:20.)

* For puzzle answers, look in the back of the book.

Woah. Looks like Memucan had a frightening case of boys-versus-girls thinking! We need a serious Truth filter to sort all of this out! And you better believe we will be seeking advice from God and His Word.

Look at Genesis 1:27 again. Write the two kinds of people who reflect God's image below.

M ____ ____ ____ and **F** ____ ____ ____ ____ ____

Both male and female are image bearers of God. One is not better than the other. Each is important.

Look again at Genesis 1:28. Fill in the blank:

God blessed _____.

Based on Genesis 1:27–28, put an ✖ by which of these statements seems true.

_____ The males are more important than the females.

_____ The females are more important than the males.

_____ God blessed both males and females and gave them both authority to take care of His world.

One of the big problems in Susa was a boys-versus-girls mindset!

Now, it is true that God has some instructions about husbands and wives written in the New Testament that we can read today. Of course, Paul, inspired by the Holy Spirit, wrote these words years after Esther was alive, but their principles were still true. Let's check it against Memucan's thinking.

Read these verses and underline the phrase that sounds a *little* like the advice Memucan gave to King Xerxes.

> For wives, this means submit to your husbands as to the Lord. For a husband is the head of his wife as Christ is the head of the church. He is the Savior of his body, the church. As the church submits to Christ, so you wives should submit to your husbands in everything. (Ephesians 5:22–24)

Maybe you underlined "wives . . . submit to your husbands." It is **TRUE** that women should respect and honor the leadership and worth of their husbands. **BUT** that's not the **WHOLE** Truth.

Let's keep reading the next few verses of Ephesians. Underline the things God's commands husbands to do *for* their wives.

For husbands, this means love your wives, just as Christ loved the church. He gave up his life for her to make her holy and clean, washed by the cleansing of God's word. He did this to present her to himself as a glorious church without a spot or wrinkle or any other blemish. Instead, she will be holy and without fault. In the same way, husbands ought to love their wives as they love their own bodies. For a man who loves his wife actually shows love for himself. No one hates his own body but feeds and cares for it, just as Christ cares for the church. And we are members of his body. (Ephesians 5:25–30)

Wow! Part of the way a man fulfills his purpose if he is married is to **LOVE** his wife and care for her. What a wonderful way to show that she is a worthy image bearer of God!

Memucan had a seriously bad case of "Boys Rule. Girls Drool!" As the king's adviser, he told Xerxes to use his power to control Queen Vashti instead of to protect and value her.

> **PROBLEM #4:**
> **King Xerxes had the wrong user manual,**
> **and that impacted how he viewed women.**

The king got advice based on the customs of man rather than the Truth of God's Word. He thought the boys should just rule over the girls without valuing and protecting them.

Queen Vashti does get sent away. And I can only imagine that lots of other wives got treated badly because of the bad example King Xerxes set.

God never intended men and women to be at odds with each other. Genesis 2:18 teaches us that God created women to be helpers for men. Put that with all we learned about how men are supposed to care for women, and we should be experiencing relationships of kindness and helpfulness with each other. Not fighting about who is more valuable!

Yep, there were **BIG PROBLEMS** in Susa!

But God was at work.

You see, God did love and bless women. He did not forget His plan for men and women to be co-rulers of the earth. And the God who provides for us all was about to set things straight . . . USING A GIRL **AND** A GUY!

In our next lesson, we'll get to meet the shero and hero in this incredible story. But first, let's ZERO IN!

ZERO IN: What does it mean?

Lots of people today have a boys-versus-girls mindset. They don't consult God's user manual to understand the words *male* or *female*. Sometimes men treat women badly. And sometimes women treat men badly. They believe the lie that their gender is more important than the other. That's very sad to me. And, just like Vashti, I say "no" to some things. For example, I do not like "Girls Rule. Boys Drool." T-shirts.

Write about one way you see boys disrespecting girls.

_____

_____

_____

Write about one way you see girls disrespecting boys.

_____

_____

_____

Another lie people sometimes believe is: "There's no difference between boys and girls." That's not true. God made us different. Guys usually have bigger heads, hearts, and lungs! We both have cartilage around our voice boxes, but boys have a lot more so it produces a bump called an "Adam's apple." Girls, of course, can have babies. Boys cannot. It's OK to admit that some things about us are different. Because they are. That doesn't mean we have different value in God's eyes, though.

Conversations about being male and female are as complicated today as they were in King Xerxes's day. Lots of people are consulting the wrong user's manual. They are looking at governmental laws and customs or the culture instead of God for counsel. For the record, most of Susa did not follow the one true God, including King Xerxes. (But you probably had already guessed that by his very bad behavior!)

I think an important lesson we can zero in on today is this: you need godly advisers who will help you.

Who are some wise people in your life who love their Bibles that you could ask for advice?

_____

_____

_____

_____

How do you know when the wise people in your life are helping to point you to your purpose? Do you know what we have today that tells us the Truth? (Hint: We've been talking about it a lot.) It's the Bible! If your wise friends are bringing you back to God's Word, there is a good chance you can trust their advice.

Circle the word *plans* and *advisers.*

Plans go wrong for lack of advice; but many advisers bring success. (Proverbs 15:22)

Now use those words to fill this sentence in to see a good equation to live by.

P_____ + **A**_____ = established purpose

ZIP IT UP: What does God want me to do with it?

It's time to *zip it up*! How can you respond to God after reading about the boys-versus-girls problems in Susa? Do you see any of those problems in your life?

Or maybe you just really don't know what your purpose is, but you want to know! One way we can seek God's counsel is to pray and ask for Him to help us think, understand the Bible, and find the right people to advise us. We can also pray for His providence to show up in our stories!

Write a prayer in the space below asking God for help with any boy-versus-girl problems in your world. Or you could write a prayer asking Him to help you understand your purpose.

When you trust God to direct your path, He can use your life too! When you make it your goal to make God famous and obey His commands, He will lead you into your purpose.

Good work, True Girl! You just studied really hard, and I'm proud of you!

In our next lesson, we're going to meet **A GIRL** named Esther and **A GUY** named Mordecai who God used to do something incredibly courageous and important. You will begin to see that it's so much better when we work together as girls and guys!

CHAPTER 2

✳ God Will Invite You into His Plan

The lobby of my church looked like a foreign country!

I had always loved the missions conference week at my church. But now, at the age of eight, I sensed that it was going to be super special this year.

There was a grass hut and a two-wheeled carriage called a *rickshaw* filling the space. When I arrived, there was an actual real missionary standing near the hut offering fruits and vegetables to taste.

That night, the missionary told us about her important work for God in India. She talked about riding in rickshaws instead of taxis. And there was a story of being invited to eat a monkey's paws. *Whoa!* My favorite part was when she used photographs on the big screen to introduce us to people who came to know Jesus. And it was all because of her important work. I thought she had the best job in the whole world.

After all her amazing stories, she said *anyone* could serve Jesus like she did.

Anyone? I thought. *What if I'm only eight years old?*

"It doesn't even matter how old you are," said the missionary. "God wants you to obey His purpose and plan for your life."

My heart skipped a beat!

I looked around at all the flags of the nations hanging up in our church. And I knew God was calling me. I awkwardly walked toward the front of the church. Then, I kneeled and prayed a simple prayer. I told the Lord I would be whatever He wanted, but I hoped it would be a Bible teacher or missionary.

Fast-forward to today. Guess what? I *am* a Bible teacher and a missionary!

I'm teaching you about the Bible right now. And I have gotten to travel to exciting places like Zambia, South Africa, Peru, Ecuador, the Dominican Republic, and Mexico to teach the Bible. So, I'm a missionary too.

It's time to learn Purpose Lesson #2, but let's review our first one. Go back to the Purpose Lessons page at the beginning of this book. Find the Purpose Lesson #1 and write it below:

⭐ PURPOSE LESSON #1 _____

_____

I was eight years old when I started to think about God's plan and purpose for my life. But here's a super big question: When do you think God started thinking about it?

Read the next verse to answer that question. It was written by Jeremiah. God's purpose for his life was to be a prophet.

Underline the words that tell you when God chose for Jeremiah to be a prophet.

"I knew you before I formed you in your mother's womb. Before you were born I set you apart and appointed you as my prophet to the nations." (Jeremiah 1:5)

Before Jeremiah was born, God decided he would be a prophet. That was Jeremiah's special purpose. It was how he would make God famous. We can assume that God also thought about my special purpose before I was born, even though I didn't know about it until I was eight!

So how can you know what God's been thinking about *you*? In this chapter, we're going to study *how* to discover God's purpose for your life.

It's time for PURPOSE LESSON #2:
You don't have to find your purpose because God will invite you into His plan.

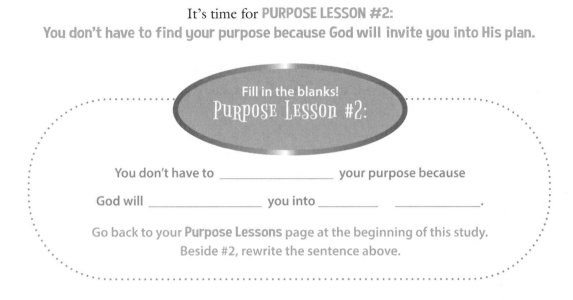

Fill in the blanks!
PURPOSE LESSON #2:

You don't have to _____ your purpose because

God will _____ you into _____ _____.

Go back to your **Purpose Lessons** page at the beginning of this study.
Beside #2, rewrite the sentence above.

OK, God doesn't email you a special invitation or send you something in the mail. But there are some ways He invites you into His plan.

In the last lesson, we dug into the BIBLE to learn about our overall purpose to make God famous. And we learned that the Bible is our instruction manual. This is where understanding your purpose always begins.

As we study the book of Esther in this lesson, we'll begin to see how God uses CIRCUMSTANCES (or the situations we find ourselves in) to direct us to our purpose.

You'll also see that Esther leans on WISE ADVISERS to make decisions about how to understand and respond to her circumstances.

At the end of this lesson, I'll share a bit about how God uses PRAYER to invite us into our purpose.

It's time to start zooming.

Zoom In & Out—Who? What? Where? When? Why?

It's time to zoom in and meet Esther. She is the heroine of the book. She's about to get an invitation. It might look like it's from King Xerxes, but if you think that, you should probably look again!

ZOOM IN!

ESTHER 2:1-8

Grab a royal-colored pencil such as purple or blue or gold. As you read the passage below, circle anything important you learn about Esther.

1 But after Xerxes' anger had subsided, he began thinking about Vashti and what she had done and the decree he had made. *2* So his personal attendants suggested, "Let us search the empire to find beautiful young virgins for the king. *3* Let the king appoint agents in each province to bring these beautiful young women into the royal harem at the fortress of Susa. Hegai, the king's eunuch in charge of the harem,* will see that they are all given beauty treatments.

4 After that, the young woman who most pleases the king will be made queen instead of Vashti." This advice was very appealing to the king, so he put the plan into effect. *5* At that time there was a Jewish man in the fortress of Susa whose name was Mordecai son of Jair. He was from the tribe of Benjamin and was a descendant of Kish and Shimei. *6* His family had been among those who, with King Jehoiachin of Judah, had been exiled from Jerusalem to Babylon by King Nebuchadnezzar. *7* This man had a very beautiful and lovely young cousin, Hadassah,

> *A **harem** is the separate part of a house or palace where women who served the king in various ways lived.

who was also called Esther. When her father and mother died, Mordecai adopted her into his family and raised her as his own daughter. 8 As a result of the king's decree, Esther, along with many other young women, was brought to the king's harem at the fortress of Susa and placed in Hegai's care.

In these verses, we learn quite a bit about our new friend! And someone very special to her, Mordecai, who was both her cousin and adoptive dad. (We'll come back to him soon.) But for now . . . let's review a few things we learned about Esther.

THE STAR OF OUR STORY } Using the clues below, find the words that describe Esther's **CIRCUMSTANCES**.

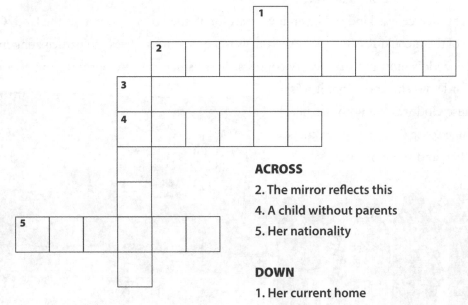

ACROSS
2. The mirror reflects this
4. A child without parents
5. Her nationality

DOWN
1. Her current home
3. Her relationship to Mordecai

* For puzzle answers, look in the back of the book.

Esther was **BEAUTIFUL**, but sadly she became an **ORPHAN** when her parents died. Thankfully, she was adopted by her older **COUSIN**, Mordecai, who took her in and treated her like his own daughter. We also find out from these verses that Esther was **JEWISH** and living in **SUSA**.

These were Esther's **CIRCUMSTANCES**. And they were about to set her up to be the **STAR** of **GOD'S STORY**!

The star of God's story

In the ancient Persian language, Esther was a word that meant "star." It's a pretty fitting name for her.

You might remember, the **CIRCUMSTANCES** were looking pretty dark when we studied the first chapter of this book of the Bible. There were big problems in Susa because King Xerxes was not serving God, but himself. He made a pretty big mess for himself when he did not respect Queen Vashti. And now he had to look for a new queen. So, he sent out a decree.

This decree was kind of like an invitation for all the young women in the land. Only, none of them could RSVP "no." Everyone was required to say "yes" to participating in one of the world's most unusual beauty contests. And Esther was one of those young women.

Little did she know that it was because God was going to use her to shine some light in the darkness. Oh, her, and someone else.

Read the verses below. Underline any words or phrases that tell you Esther was shining like a star in Susa. (That is to say, words and phrases that tell you people saw something special in her.)

ESTHER 2:9-11

9 Hegai was very impressed with Esther and treated her kindly. He quickly ordered a special menu for her and provided her with beauty treatments. He also assigned her seven maids specially chosen from the king's palace, and he moved her and her maids into the best place in the harem. 10 Esther had not told anyone of her nationality and family background, because Mordecai had directed her not to do so. 11 Every day Mordecai would take a walk near the courtyard of the harem to find out about Esther and what was happening to her.

Esther impressed Hegai, the guy in charge of the king's girls. So, he took special care of her. He treated her with kindness, and gave her special food and beauty treatments. She even got seven maids. (I do believe she was already shining brightly like the star she was!)

Look again at verses 10 and 11 above. Write down two things that demonstrate Mordecai also cared deeply about his adopted daughter.

➤ _____

_____

_____

Mordecai had some **WISE ADVICE** for his adopted daughter! What was it? Look at verse 10 to see. Write it below.

➤ _____

_____

It's time to **zoom out** and get some important context.

ZOOM OUT!

First, let's talk about Mordecai so we can understand something very important about the CIRCUMSTANCES he (and Esther) found themselves in.

Look back at Esther 2:5. Draw a big blue star over the word that describes what kind of man Mordecai was. (You're looking for an adjective for the word *man*.)

Now circle the name of the fortress where Mordecai lived.

A Jewish man living in Susa? FULL STOP! This would have been a sentence that stood out to someone reading it back when it was originally written. These were *unusual* CIRCUMSTANCES. Let's find out why.

Turn to the map at the beginning of the book. Find the star on the page. Write "Jerusalem" beside it.

Next, draw footprints from Jerusalem to Susa.

Jerusalem was the capital of Israel, which was the special nation God gave to the Jewish people. So, why's this guy Mordecai living sooooo far away? (Those are interesting CIRCUMSTANCES, don't you think?)

The fortress of Susa was 765 miles away from Mordecai's true hometown. Today, it would take like twelve hours to drive that far. (You'd for sure be saying, "Are we there yet?" And way more than once.) But back in the day most people walked. (That's why I had you draw footprints.)

Why did Mordecai walk that far?

Well, in all likelihood, HE didn't. But his mom and dad or his grandparents might have. Because 100 years earlier, some super greedy people forced the Israelites out of their home in Jerusalem. They wanted that special land for themselves, so they tied many of the men and women up and forced them to walk to strange places like Babylon and Susa. They were *exiles*. (That's what you call someone who is forced to live outside of their homeland.) The Bible tells us that many of them were homesick.

Eventually, some Jews did get to go home to Israel, including two prophets named Ezra and Nehemiah. But some of them stayed where they'd been forced to live, including Daniel. (You know, the one who survived the lions' den. He stayed in Babylon when the Jews were finally allowed to go home.) Apparently, Mordecai either could not or did not go back to his homeland when it became possible. He stayed in Susa, the capital of Persia.

Why is it important to know this?

Well, Mordecai and his cousin, Esther, were strangers in the city where they lived along with the other Jewish people who lived there. It was not their home. They were not Persian. And the people who did consider Persia their home did not worship the one true God. This is important background information and it's why we needed to zoom out today. (These CIRCUMSTANCES also helped point them to their purpose.) Why? Well, many of the Persian people still did not like the Jewish people!

Now, Mordecai knew that some Persians were not kind to the Jews because this was not their home, so he advised Esther not to tell anyone she was Jewish. (We'll meet one of those people who did not like the Jews in chapter 4.)

He was also concerned for Esther's well-being! He made sure to swing by the palace grounds to check on her and make sure she was OK. How often? EVERY DAY!

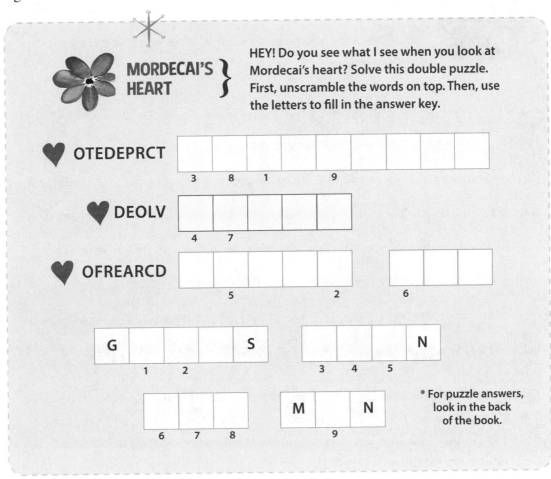

MORDECAI'S HEART

HEY! Do you see what I see when you look at Mordecai's heart? Solve this double puzzle. First, unscramble the words on top. Then, use the letters to fill in the answer key.

♥ OTEDEPRCT
3 8 1 9

♥ DEOLV
4 7

♥ OFREARCD
5 2 6

G ___ ___ ___ S ___ ___ ___ N
1 2   3 4 5

___ ___ ___ ___ M ___ N
6 7 8   9

* For puzzle answers, look in the back of the book.

The way Mordecai treated Esther sounded a lot like what men are supposed to do according to what we studied in Ephesians in chapter 1. Wow. Mordecai was a really good man!

God was beginning to invite Esther into her purpose. How? By using the CIRCUMSTANCES of her life and Mordecai's WISE ADVICE.

Let's go back to zooming in.

ZOOM IN!

ESTHER 2:15-20

Does Esther follow Mordecai's wise advice? Read the following verses. Double underline the answer.

15 Esther was the daughter of Abihail, who was Mordecai's uncle. (Mordecai had adopted his younger cousin Esther.) When it was Esther's turn to go to the king, she accepted the advice of Hegai, the eunuch in charge of the harem. She asked for nothing except what he suggested, and she was admired by everyone who saw her. 16 Esther was taken to King Xerxes at the royal palace in early winter of the seventh year of his reign. 17 And the king loved Esther more than any of the other young women. He was so delighted with her that he set the royal crown on her head and declared her queen instead of Vashti. 18 To celebrate the occasion, he gave a great banquet in Esther's honor for all his nobles and officials, declaring a public holiday for the provinces and giving generous gifts to everyone. 19 Even after all the young women had been transferred to the second harem and Mordecai had become a palace official, 20 Esther continued to keep her family background and nationality a secret. She was still following Mordecai's directions, just as she did when she lived in his home.

Esther won the unusual beauty contest and began to wear the royal crown. She enjoyed a great banquet in her honor. Does this go to her head? Nope. Verse 20 reads, "She was still following Mordecai's directions, *just as she did when she lived in his home.*"

And she needed this wise advice because what happened to her was not just unusual CIRCUMSTANCES, but evil! I mean, King Xerxes had "stranger danger" written all over him. He was *forcing* women to come compete to be his wife! That's totally creepy. But the empire he ruled was full of darkness. And he was bad through and through.

For the record, if any man in a high position of power forces you into *anything* ever, RUN! And if it's a guy who thinks all the women in the land should be "his" possessions, run faster! Then, tell a good person who can help you get that guy in trouble. Today, most countries have laws that protect women from men like King Xerxes.

But Esther lived in a different time and place. Remember, the reason she and Mordecai were there in the first place was because their parents or grandparents were forced out of their homeland, Israel. Esther entered into these strange CIRCUMSTANCES and found herself in even stranger CIRCUMSTANCES where she could not tell people who she really was—a Jew.

She might have felt invisible in spite of all the public attention. It would have been easy for her to believe the lie: *I guess I'm not a big part of God's plan now!*

Oh, but she was! Her odd CIRCUMSTANCES and Mordecai's WISE ADVICE were two of the things that God used to invite her into her purpose.

Here's something important, though: being invited into her purpose did not result in immediately doing what God planned for her to do. God still had some prep work to do on her heart.

ZERO IN: What does it mean?

As you read your BIBLE, you'll understand more about your purpose to make God famous. Then, God will use CIRCUMSTANCES to direct and lead you. Be sure to ask for WISE ADVICE from godly people. And, as we'll see in a few minutes, it's also important to PRAY for God to guide you and your advisers.

You won't know your purpose right away. But you can always be getting ready to do what God has planned for you. So, let's spend some time preparing *your* heart for *your* purpose. Esther leaves us some important purpose preparation tips.

Purpose Prep Tip #1: Be prepared to feel unseen.

Do you ever feel like you couldn't possibly have an important purpose because no one sees you? Well, I think Esther did too. I mean, she may have received a royal title and was one of the most famous women in all of Persia. But she could not tell people who she *really* was. Mordecai told her it wasn't wise to reveal her nationality. Esther may not have been safe if people knew she was Jewish, *which was one of the most important things about her.* (As the story unfolds, you'll see why it was critical that God placed one of His chosen people in the palace.)

I mean, think about how lonely it must have been for Esther. She was crowned queen and paraded in front of everyone, but at the same time no one knew what was most meaningful to her—that she was a Jewish woman who loved the one true God!

We also live in a world that does not love God. Sometimes you will have to be careful about when to stand up for God's Truth and when to wait for God's timing to be bold. This can sometimes feel a little lonely. It could feel like no one even sees you.

Have you ever felt lonely or unseen because you were the one who believed in God? Or have you felt like you had to hide the fact that you are a Christian? Write about that time below.

If you have not felt that kind of loneliness before, let me encourage you to be prepared for it. But during that time, God will help your heart learn and grow. You can use this space to write a prayer asking for strength.

Purpose Prep Tip #2: Purpose requires patience.

Esther didn't just show up and become queen. First, she had to grow up into a lovely young woman. Then, she had to participate in a full year of preparation.

I didn't start to be a Bible teacher or missionary the day I prayed about that when I was eight. I also had to grow up. And then, I attended college to learn to write and communicate better. After that, it was almost *ten more years* until I wrote my first book.

What I'm saying is this: be patient! Do everything you do right now as if you're studying for what God has planned for you to do in the future. But try to enjoy the pace. It's going to be slow.

One thing you can do now to better understand your purpose is read your Bible every day. I began to do this when I was eight years old—the same year I sensed God calling me to be a Bible teacher or a missionary.

You can start to read your Bible regularly too. Use the calendar below to schedule out your Bible reading time for the next week. (It can include your Bible study time with this book!)

As you become more familiar with your Bible, you'll be more confident when CIRCUMSTANCES and WISE ADVISERS help you see God's invitation to your purpose.

Purpose Prep Tip #3: Accept WISE ADVICE.

There will be times when you don't know what to do or how to do it. Esther faced one of those times when her year of preparation was over and she was about to meet King Xerxes. She probably didn't know how to approach the king. After all, she'd never done something like that before.

Turn back to the page at the front of the book labeled "My Notes On Esther." I think you're ready to write in some information about Mordecai. He's labeled "Her Uncle." Add his name and write down what you know about him.

ESTHER 2:15b

Read Esther 2:15b. Circle what Esther asked to take with her.

15 When it was Esther's turn to go to the king, she accepted the advice of Hegai, the eunuch in charge of the harem. She asked for nothing except what he suggested, and she was admired by everyone who saw her.

When it was Esther's turn to visit the king, she was able to choose whatever she wanted to take with her! But instead of making the decision by herself, she accepted advice from Hegai.

Remember Hegai? He was in charge of helping women prepare to meet the king and oversaw all of Esther's beauty treatments. And he was impressed with Esther from the very beginning. He had treated her kindly and wanted to see her succeed! He knew King Xerxes better than Esther. So, he chose clothes that would help bring her favor with the king.

As you are growing in wisdom, there will be people in your life who offer advice.

In the verse below, cross out the word used to describe someone who does not listen to advice from others. Circle the word used to describe someone who listens to others.

 Fools think their own way is right,
but the wise listen to others. (Proverbs 12:15)

In the last chapter, I told you to write a list of people who could advise you. But I'm seeing an important theme here! In that chapter, I told you to **SEEK** advice. This time, I'm suggesting it's a good idea to **LISTEN** to it while you're waiting for your purpose to unfold.

Let's zip this lesson up!

ZIP IT UP: What does God want me to do with it?

Right now, you might have a lot of dreams or thoughts about what you **WANT** to do with your life. This is your "will" or desire. But I'll bet God's cooking up some master plan that is better than you could even ask for. How can you know what God's plan and purpose is for your life? You can pray. But let's look at *how* to pray.

In Matthew 6, we read how Jesus told us to pray. Circle whose will is to "be done on earth."

 Pray like this: Our Father in heaven, may your name be kept holy. May your Kingdom come soon. May your will be done on earth, as it is in heaven. (Matthew 6:9–10)

Today, I want to challenge you to give your dreams to God. Tell Him what you want, but then let Him hold your dreams in His hands. When you surrender your plans to Him, He will do more than you could ever ask or think. And He can help you see how your desires fit into His will.

Let's end our study time today by praying the way Jesus instructed. Using Matthew 6:9–10 as an example, write a prayer that expresses your desire to do God's will on earth.

_____

_____

_____

_____

_____

_____

_____

_____

_____

_____

Good work, True Girl! I pray that God's will on earth will be done through your life.

Well, we've gotten a pretty good introduction to Esther and some of the people in her life, including the very wise and good Mordecai. (He's going to become very important!) But there's one more person we still need to meet. Come back soon to learn about someone in the story who was **NOT** walking in God's purpose.

CHAPTER 3

When You're Discouraged About Your Purpose, God Is Not

Imagine this: It's your favorite night of the week because it's family movie night. You've thankfully just completed your last word problem in your math homework when you hear your mom shouting from the kitchen.

"Hey! Am I gonna watch this movie alone tonight?"

You slap your three-ring binder shut, jump off your bed, and open your bedroom door. *Ah!* The smell of fresh buttered popcorn greets you.

As you walk down the hall you remember: It's Dad's turn to pick the movie. *What will it be?*

"Hey, Cupcake!" says Dad when you arrive just in time to see him push the remote-control button with his thumb. Then, there on the screen is the answer to your question: *The Super Mario Bros. Movie.*

Figures! Back in the day, Dad was one of the contenders for the highest Super Mario Bros. score ever. His dreams were dashed when Andrew Gardikis scored 1,435,100 points on January 8, 2015.[2] Dad has told you the story over and over.

You can just hear him solemnly saying, "And that's the day I retired my Nintendo game console."

The movie's not so bad. Actually, you like it a lot . . . but right at the beginning the bad guy shows up. The monstrous Bowser has mad fire-breathing skills and a full-throated roar. He tries to force Princess Peach to marry him. He wants to **DISCOURAGE** her by making her think she cannot rule her own kingdom peacefully.

Will Mario rescue her?

Will Princess Peach continue to rule the Mushroom Kingdom?

Most every movie we watch reminds us that life is a battle between the good guys and the bad guys. Of course, many of the plotlines are made-up stories, but the battle between good and evil is **REAL**. As a matter of fact, it started allllllll the way back in Genesis.

God created a perfect world. His purpose was to have a relationship with the people that He created. Adam and Eve were living in the garden and never experienced pain or hunger or sadness. That's the way God wanted it.

But Satan was jealous of God. He wanted to make himself famous *instead* of God. (Hey, that sounds a lot like King Xerxes!) So, Satan went down into the garden in the form of a snake. He intended to **DISCOURAGE** Eve from following God's plan.

Of course, the snake succeeded. Eve ate the fruit from the tree God told her not to eat from. She disobeyed God.

God punished the snake for tempting her by taking away its legs. (Yes, snakes used to have legs.) Then, God told Satan this:

 I'm declaring war between you and the Woman, between your offspring and hers. (Genesis 3:15a MSG)

From that point on, there has been good and evil in our world. And those forces are at constant war.

True Girl, if you discover God's plan for your life, that is good. So, you can be sure there will be forces that fight against it. And that is bad.

But before we get to that, let's refresh your memory on the lessons we've learned so far. Can you fill in the blanks? (If you need a little help, remember that you already wrote these on your Purpose Lessons page at the beginning of the book. You can always turn there for help!)

⭐ **PURPOSE LESSON #1** _____

_____

⭐ **PURPOSE LESSON #2** _____

_____

It's time to explore **PURPOSE LESSON #3:**
When you're discouraged about your purpose, God is not.

Fill in the blanks!
PURPOSE LESSON #3:

When you are _____

about your _____ God is _____.

Go back to your **Purpose Lessons** page at the beginning of this study.
Beside #3, rewrite the sentence above.

There will be times when you feel really discouraged as you discover and live out God's purpose for your life. That's when you have to persevere.

What's *perseverance*? Here's a simple definition of the word:

{ **perseverance: the ability to keep doing something in spite of obstacles** }

Why do we need perseverance to do what God planned for us to do? Because Satan has plans to discourage you.

Does that make you want to put this book back on the shelf for good? Hear me out. You need to understand **WHY** we face discouragement *and*—here's the best part—**WHAT** you can do about it.

Buckle up as we start zooming.

→ Zoom In & Out—Who? What? Where? When? Why?

You're about to meet a bad guy. It's time to jump back into our story and learn about the biggest, baddest guy in Susa. (Maybe even worse than King Xerxes.)

ZOOM IN!

ESTHER 3:1-2

Underline the name of the guy King Xerxes promoted to the most powerful position in the land of Susa. Be sure to include this man's full six-word title.

1 Some time later King Xerxes promoted Haman son of Hammedatha the Agagite over all the other nobles, making him the most powerful official in the empire. 2 All the king's officials would bow down before Haman to show him respect whenever he passed by, for so the king had commanded. But Mordecai refused to bow down or show him respect.

Haman was the bad guy.

What did the king command people to do when Haman walked by?

_____

_____

Who did not obey that command?

>———➤ **M**_____

Hmm . . . I wonder why Mordecai didn't do what everyone else was doing? Let's investigate! We'll start by learning more about Haman.

Write below what people group Haman was from. (Hint: It starts with an A.)

>———➤ **A**_____

Haman was an **AGAGITE**, which was a group of people that were part of the Amalekite people group. Is that important? Well, it must be or the Bible would not have included it. But what does it tell us?

When you are studying the Bible and wonder what something means, that's a good invitation to zoom out! So, let's do that. As we learn why it is important that Haman was an **AGAGITE**, we'll also learn more about why it was wise for Esther to hide the fact that she was a **JEW**.

ZOOM OUT!

The Old Testament is the first half of the Bible, written before Jesus was born. When you read it, you'll notice that God protects the Jewish people. That's because they were His special chosen family. Jesus was eventually going to be born through a Jewish woman.

FULL STOP! Look back at that verse about the battle between good and evil, Genesis 3:15a. It's the one near the boxing gloves.

Circle the word **offspring** in Genesis 3:15a.

Jesus would be the *offspring* of the woman. That means He'd be the child of a woman in the Jewish family. The war declared in the garden of Eden would be won when Jesus was born.

So, Satan took every chance he could get to **DISCOURAGE** anyone who was part of the plan to bring Jesus into the world. Since he didn't know who would be the mother of Jesus, he just tried to wipe out all of the Jewish people. To do that, Satan had to stir up anger and hatred in other people groups. So, throughout the Old Testament we see lots of people groups that wanted to wipe out the Jewish people so Jesus could never be born.

FIND THE ENEMIES OF THE JEWISH PEOPLE

} In this word search, I've buried the names of some of the people groups who were enemies of God's Jewish family. Can you find them?

CANAANITES   PHILISTINES   AMALEKITES   BABYLONIANS   ASSYRIANS

```
D  A  J  P  S  H  U  A  Z  F  W  V  E  A  Y
D  C  W  A  H  V  J  P  F  D  C  O  T  S  B
R  J  A  O  B  I  U  D  F  B  F  S  K  S  V
A  H  X  N  R  X  L  J  L  Z  V  O  H  Y  J
M  M  R  S  A  O  M  I  K  T  F  P  A  R  G
A  T  W  J  L  A  Y  G  S  S  P  N  V  I  Q
L  D  Q  V  L  Z  N  T  Q  T  D  F  C  A  D
E  I  K  L  U  T  K  I  Q  J  I  X  T  N  G
K  D  B  R  D  L  U  Z  T  N  I  N  U  S  G
I  F  R  X  N  Q  E  S  G  E  H  Y  E  H  Z
T  X  T  I  U  V  R  C  W  R  S  J  K  S  A
E  W  K  T  V  Z  K  I  I  E  O  A  J  V  S
S  M  B  A  B  Y  L  O  N  I  A  N  S  B  K
W  X  V  U  Q  L  J  A  H  K  E  I  V  M  Q
A  B  J  K  I  D  F  B  E  Q  G  F  F  N  F
```

*For puzzle answers, look in the back of the book.

Write the people group below that would have been most important to Haman.

A _____

Ya starting to see what I see?

Five hundred years before Esther was born, a battle between the Amalekites and the Jewish people was in full swing. The Amalekites were some of the most evil people on the earth. The things they did to the Jews were so terrible I cannot even write them here. They tortured, abused, and killed God's special people over and over again. They were Satan's tool to **DISCOURAGE** the Jews who believed in and pursued God's plan.

Eventually, God said, "Enough!" He sent a special message to Saul, the king of the Jewish people.

Circle the verbs (or action words) that describe what King Saul was instructed by God to do.

 Now go and completely destroy the entire Amalekite nation.
(1 Samuel 15:3)

Underline the adverb that describes the extent of destruction God commanded.

Completely destroy. Does that sound horrible? It does to me too. But God had been patient with the Amalekites for a long time. He finally gave King Saul a command to destroy them.

Here's the problem. King Saul only *sort of* obeyed God's instructions.

In the verses below, circle the name of the one person King Saul did not completely destroy.

 Then Saul slaughtered the Amalekites from Havilah all the way to Shur, east of Egypt. He captured Agag, the Amalekite king, but completely destroyed everyone else. Saul and his men spared Agag's life and kept the best of the sheep and goats, the cattle, the fat calves, and the lambs— everything, in fact, that appealed to them. They destroyed only what was worthless or of poor quality. (1 Samuel 15:7–9)

Compare the name of the king that Saul kept alive to Haman's big six-word title in Esther 3:1. What can you guess based on comparing these two verses in the Bible?

_____

_____

Congratulations! You just did some super hard zooming. Did you figure out that Haman was one of the great-great-great-great-grandsons of Agag, king of the Amalekites?

Haman was one of the greatest enemies of God's special people.

King Saul's disobedience caused problems for the Jewish people MANY years later when Esther and her people were forced to live in Persia. The Agagites, descendants of the Amelekites, were still alive. And Satan was *still* using them to discourage God's people who believed and pursued God's plan.

Is it starting to make sense why Mordecai advised Esther not to reveal that she was Jewish? Pick your answer.

_____NO, I don't get it. It seemed like everyone should just be friends.

_____YES, revealing her nationality would be dangerous for Esther.

The correct answer is *yes* because Mordecai knew it would be dangerous for anyone to discover that they were Jewish.

There was just one problem. The king's new rule about bowing down to Haman was the very thing that could blow their cover! Obeying King Xerxes rule to bow down to Haman would require any Jewish person to *disobey* one of God's Ten Commandments for the Jewish people.

Circle which one of the Ten Commandments a Jew would have to disobey to honor King Xerxes' new command.

1 Have no other gods but God.

2 Do not bow down and worship any other god.

3 Be careful with God's name.

4 Keep the Sabbath day special.

5 Honor your father and mother.

6 Do not murder.

7 Keep your marriage promises.

8 Do not steal.

9 Do not lie.

10 Do not covet.

Mordecai knew he could only bow to God Himself. So, he refused to bow to Haman. But that turned out to be dangerous. Let's go back to zooming in to see why.

ZOOM IN!

ESTHER 3:3-6

Underline what Haman learned about Mordecai when he refused to bow down.

3 Then the palace officials at the king's gate asked Mordecai, "Why are you disobeying the king's command?" 4 They spoke to him day after day, but still he refused to comply with the order. So they spoke to Haman about this to see if he would tolerate Mordecai's conduct, since Mordecai had told them he was a Jew. 5 When Haman saw that Mordecai would not bow down or show him respect, he was filled with rage. 6 He had learned of Mordecai's nationality, so he decided it was not enough to lay hands on Mordecai alone. Instead, he looked for a way to destroy all the Jews throughout the entire empire of Xerxes.

A *nationality* is another name for a people group. Haman now knew that Mordecai was Jewish.

Circle the words in the passage we just read that tell us how Haman felt about not being worshiped by Mordecai.

He was angrier than Bowser when Princess Peach refused to marry him in *The Super Mario Bros. Movie*!

ESTHER 3:7-15

As you read the next passage, underline the things Haman wanted to do to the Jewish people because of how angry he was.

7 So in the month of April, during the twelfth year of King Xerxes' reign, lots were cast in Haman's presence (the lots were called purim) to determine the best day and month to take action. And the day selected was March 7, nearly a year later. 8 Then Haman approached King Xerxes and said, "There is a certain race of people scattered through all the provinces of your empire who keep themselves separate from everyone else. Their laws are different from those of any other people, and they refuse to obey the laws of the king. So it is not in the king's interest to let them live. 9 If it please the king, issue a decree that they be destroyed, and I will give 10,000 large sacks of silver to the government administrators to be deposited in the royal treasury." 10 The king agreed, confirming his decision by removing his signet ring from his finger and giving it to Haman son of Hammedatha the Agagite, the enemy of the Jews. 11 The king said, "The money and the people are both yours to do with as you see fit." 12 So on April 17 the king's secretaries were summoned, and a decree was written exactly as Haman dictated. It was sent to the king's highest officers, the governors of the respective provinces, and the nobles of each province in their own scripts and languages. The decree was written in the name of King Xerxes and sealed with the king's signet ring. 13 Dispatches were sent by swift messengers into all the provinces of the empire, giving the order that all Jews—

young and old, including women and children—must be killed, slaughtered, and annihilated on a single day. This was scheduled to happen on March 7 of the next year. The property of the Jews would be given to those who killed them. *14* A copy of this decree was to be issued as law in every province and proclaimed to all peoples, so that they would be ready to do their duty on the appointed day. *15* At the king's command, the decree went out by swift messengers, and it was also proclaimed in the fortress of Susa. Then the king and Haman sat down to drink, but the city of Susa fell into confusion.

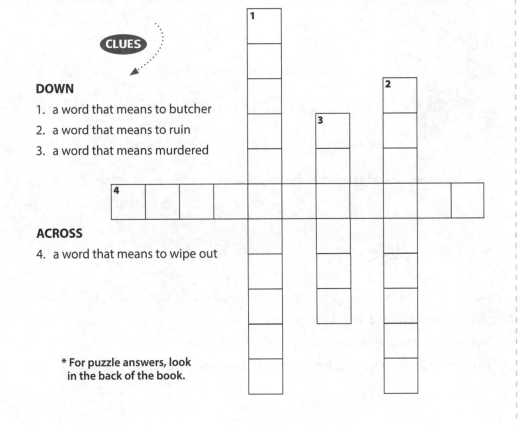

DISCOURAGING DISCOURSE

The words Haman used to describe what would happen to the Jewish people were horribly discouraging. What were they?

CLUES

DOWN

1. a word that means to butcher
2. a word that means to ruin
3. a word that means murdered

ACROSS

4. a word that means to wipe out

* For puzzle answers, look in the back of the book.

I feel like we should stop for a moment. Sometimes we get so used to the bad guys in movies that we forget how truly scary it would have been for real people to face a threat like this. Take a deep breath. (Sigh!) It's OK to feel troubled right now. This is very serious stuff.

Let's keep learning because the story does end well.

Once Haman got the king to agree to his DISCOURAGING plan, he needed a way to make sure nothing could stop it. So, he got the king to give him his signet ring.

Signet Rings

In ancient Persia, a signet ring worked just like a signature. Each ring had a picture or symbol to represent the person who owned it. Wax was poured onto important papers and the signet ring was pressed into the hot liquid, leaving the "signature" of the person who approved of the words on the document. It was kind of like a stamp of approval.

ESTHER 4:1-3

Let's read one more piece of the book of Esther today. Grab a blue pencil or pen. Use it to draw tears above each word that tells you that Mordecai and all the Jewish people in Susa were discouraged.

1 When Mordecai learned about all that had been done, he tore his clothes, put on burlap and ashes, and went out into the city, crying with a loud and bitter wail. 2 He went as far as the gate of the palace, for no one was allowed to enter the palace gate while wearing clothes of mourning. 3 And as news of the king's decree reached all the provinces, there was great mourning among the Jews. They fasted, wept, and wailed, and many people lay in burlap and ashes.

We just zoomed through an awful lot of discouragement! Can you imagine how Mordecai must have felt? Yes! Discouraged.

But he (and Esther) *persevered* through this hard time.

Do you know who wasn't discouraged in this story? God.

Even when we face incredible discouragement and it feels like everything is falling apart, ····▶ God is still in control.

Look back at Esther 3:7–15. Find the blue words and read them again. Fill in the blanks below to record what Haman did before he took his evil plan to King Xerxes.

In the month of April, Haman cast _____ to determine when to

execute his evil plan. These _____ were actually dice that were

called _____ . The lots told Haman to take action on

_____ 7th, almost a full _____ later.

Casting lots was a way a lot of people in the Old Testament made decisions. It was a little bit like flipping a coin to decide which team gets the ball at the beginning of a soccer game. That's an OK way to start a friendly athletic competition, but it's not how God wants us to make wise choices. (We learned in the last chapter what tools to use for making decisions: the Bible, prayer, circumstances, and wise advisers.)

The Old Testament has a Bible verse to remind people that even when they use faulty methods of making decisions, God is still in control.

Cross out the part of the verse below that is about lots. Circle the part that tells us who is in control of every decision.

 The lot is cast into the lap, but its every decision is from the LORD. (Proverbs 16:33 NIV)

Haman was not in control of the Jewish people. God was! In fact, the way Haman's dice fell helped the Jewish people. **It gave them almost an ENTIRE YEAR to respond before Haman would carry out his evil plan.**

Whew! Finally, some good news in this lesson. I think that's a good place to stop zooming.

ZERO IN: What does it mean?

Have you ever felt discouraged?

I have.

Once I was sitting in a meeting room with a pen in my hand, trying not to cry in front of a whole bunch of people. The paper in front of me had so many fancy legal words on it that I hardly understood. But I knew what signing my name on them meant. My ministry for tween girls would cease to exist.

You see, the True Girl ministry was only a few years old when I got the breakthrough of a lifetime. It was a great big three-year contract to write all kinds of books for girls. There would be Bible studies (like this one) and fiction books and all sorts of wonderful tools to help girls love Jesus and their Bibles! My little growing ministry was going to reach more tween girls than I could have ever asked or imagined.

But then . . .

The company that offered me that agreement hired someone new. She didn't see the same potential in True Girl. Or me.

The papers in front of me would erase the previous agreement. No books. No Bible studies.

I would have just the one existing book and that didn't feel like a ministry at all. Just one book. My emotions were telling me this was the end and I was so sad.

But I didn't have a choice. I had to sign this.

As I put my pen to the paper, I felt the tears forming. After a sloppy signature, I excused myself with all the dignity I could muster.

Then, I went to the bathroom and cried.

But after that meeting, I *persevered*!

Even though I was discouraged, I knew that God was not. He was in control. If He wanted me to minister to girls, He would find new ways and I would follow Him.

Write about a time when you were discouraged or something you are discouraged about right now.

_____

_____

_____

_____

_____

_____

_____

What's a girl to do?

Well, first of all:

It's OK to cry when you are discouraged.

Mordecai cried when he was discouraged. I did. You can too. Don't let anyone tell you that it's not appropriate to grieve when life gets discouraging.

But we also need to remember:

God is not discouraged. He is in control.

When we remember that God is in control, we will be confident in discouraging circumstances. And that's what enables us to persevere.

But wait? How can you be crying and confident at the same time. Glad ya asked! I can help with that.

First, look back at Esther 4:1–3 and find the word **fasting**. Put a square around it.

Fasting? What's that? **Fasting** is a spiritual discipline that is taught in the Bible. Jesus expected His followers to fast, and He said that God rewards fasting. Fasting, according to the Bible, is a special time of intense prayer during which someone eats less. They basically spend a lot of extra time in prayer talking to God about special needs or problems in their life. (For the record, the purpose of a fast is praying, not being hungry. So, if someone just stops eating but doesn't pray, they're just on a diet!)

You might wonder, *Why can't they eat while they pray?* Well, practically, if they're not eating, they have more time to pray. But more importantly, the Bible indicates that eating less is a way of humbling oneself in neediness and helplessness before God (Psalm 69:10; Psalm 35:13; Ezra 8:21).

Please don't try fasting unless you talk to your mom about it first! Your body is still growing and needs lots of nutrients to be healthy. And there are some people who should never fast due to special health concerns. But under the right guidance and at the right time, a godly older woman like your mom could help you learn more about fasting.

Fill in the blank.

Mordecai and all the Jewish people were not just wailing and crying, they were also fasting. This meant they were p ____ ____ ____ ____ ____ ____ to God.

Mordecai and the other Jewish people started praying when they were discouraged. And because their lives were in danger, they went the extra step to humble themselves with a fast. This was their way of saying, "God, we *really* need You!" They were crying out to Him for help.

Did God hear them? Read the verses below. Use a blue pen to draw tears above all the words that give us permission to cry.

You keep track of all my sorrows. You have collected all my tears in your bottle. You have recorded each one in your book. My enemies will retreat when I call to you for help. This I know: God is on my side! (Psalm 56:8–9)

Now, use a red pen to draw hearts above the words that give us cause to be confident.

The Bible tells us exactly what to do when we feel like everything is falling apart. Cry out to God for help! This is how we persevere—most of the time.

There are times when things falling apart is God's message to redirect your life. How can you know the difference? Well, we learned in chapter 2 that God invites us into His purpose for our lives through the Bible, prayer, circumstances, and godly advisers. When we face discouragement, we can use those same resources to help us to know if we are staying in God's purpose.

Remember that discouraging situation you wrote about a few minutes ago? Let's make a plan for you!

In the lines below, write down your answers to each question. If you need help with this, ask an adult. (You may need to ask one of your godly advisers about your problem anyway!)

What does the BIBLE say?

⟫⟶ _____

_____

_____

What are the CIRCUMSTANCES of your life revealing?

⟫⟶ _____

_____

_____

What do your GODLY ADVISERS say?

⟫⟶ _____

_____

_____

You may be in the middle of crying out to God for this hard thing. And it hurts a lot. But God does have a good plan. Let me encourage you by telling you how that whole situation with my publisher ended up. You know, the one where I lost the contract for three years of books?

Well, I kept crying out to God for my little ministry for tween girls. And He kept blessing me. One little opportunity at a time. Not only did I find a new publisher, but the old publisher came back to me and said, "Hey, let's do more stuff together!"

As for True Girl, it's grown and grown. We now have live events, online Bible studies, a subscription box, and a great podcast. We serve girls in 130 countries.

Nothing gets in the way of God's plan!

So, if you're feeling discouraged right now, remember that and keep crying out to God. Be faithful one day at a time.

OK, the last tool you need to use is **PRAYER**. So, let's **zip it up**!

 ZIP IT UP: What does God want me to do with it?

Let's start today by meditating on and remembering a time when God answered a prayer you were praying during a difficult time *in the past*. I want you to do this so you can build up your faith and confidence in the truth that He does hear us when we pray. (Because we're about to pray for your difficult time that's happening *right now*.)

Psalm 56:9 tells us to call out to God when we are discouraged. That's what I want you to do right now. Write a prayer asking God to help you believe that He is on your side.

You remember that the Jewish people had almost an entire year to respond to Haman's evil plan, right? That little detail is going to prove to be very interesting in our studies ahead. Come back next time to see how Mordecai gets Esther to be a part of it all.

✳ God's Purpose May Require You to Do Things You Don't Want to Do

Amy Carmichael wanted blue eyes. Her mother told her God answers our prayers. For many years, Amy asked God to change her brown eyes to blue. And she believed He could do it. She often checked in the mirror just to see if He had answered her prayer.

But He never did.

As a little girl, Amy didn't have a clue what God had planned for her. But by the time she was a teen, she wanted to go to the mission field and thought about it all the time.

Eventually, she did end up being a missionary in India. It was there that she finally learned why God made her with brown eyes. Amy helped young girls escape from slavery, and it was dangerous work. To be safe, she had to look like an Indian women. If she had been born with blue eyes, there would be no way anyone would believe she was really from India.[3]

The women of India had brown eyes!

Amy Carmichael obviously understood why God wanted hers to be brown too!

God's purpose may require you to accept things about yourself. (I, for example, wanted to be an elementary school teacher, by my brain doesn't do math well. I had to accept that and change my career path to communication and being a Bible teacher. So glad I did!)

God's purpose may also require you to *do* things you don't want to. And that's what Esther's life is going to show us today! Obeying God isn't always easy.

But before I tell you today's purpose lesson, let's review. If you need help, remember check out your Purpose Lessons page at the beginning of the book!

⭐ **PURPOSE LESSON #1** _____

_____

⭐ **PURPOSE LESSON #2** _____

_____

⭐ **PURPOSE LESSON #3** _____

_____

And now for **PURPOSE LESSON #4:**

God's purpose may require you to do things you don't want to do.

Fill in the blanks!

PURPOSE LESSON #4:

God's _____ may _____ you to

_____ _____ _____ _____ _____ to do.

Go back to your **Purpose Lessons** page at the beginning of this study.
Beside #4, rewrite the sentence above.

Sometimes following God's plan for your life is difficult. It was that way for Esther. Remember where we left off in her story?

The city of Susa was in a state of confusion as they heard the news that all the Jews were in terrible danger. The news had spread all over Susa, and Mordecai was fasting and weeping and wailing. (A lot of the Jews were.)

But there was one person who hadn't heard: Esther.

What would she do when she learned that her people were doomed?

ZOOM IN!

ESTHER 4:4-9

Let's start by reading **just** the first verse below. Find a gray pencil or pen. Use it to draw a cloud above the word that describes Esther's emotion when she heard that Mordecai was wearing burlap and ashes and crying in the streets.

4 When Queen Esther's maids and eunuchs came and told her about Mordecai, she was deeply distressed. She sent clothing to him to replace the burlap, but he refused it. **5** Then Esther sent for Hathach, one of the king's eunuchs who had been appointed as her attendant. She ordered him to go to Mordecai and find out what was troubling him and why he was in mourning. **6** So Hathach went out to Mordecai in the square in front of the palace gate. **7** Mordecai told him the whole story, including the exact amount of money Haman had promised to pay into the royal treasury for the destruction of the Jews. **8** Mordecai gave Hathach a copy of the decree issued in Susa that called for the death of all Jews. He asked Hathach to show it to Esther and explain the situation to her. He also asked Hathach to direct her to go to the king to beg for mercy and plead for her people.

9 So Hathach returned to Esther with Mordecai's message.

Esther hadn't even heard that God's special people were in trouble, only that her adoptive dad was wearing burlap and ashes. But she was *distressed*. That means she was suffering emotionally. Why?

Well, it was a tradition in Esther's time to put on scratchy clothing and cover yourself in ashes when you were mourning. This was kind of like people today wearing black to a funeral. What people wear can show what they feel on the inside—sadness and despair.

Based on that little history lesson, why do you think Esther was distressed **before** she even heard about the bad news?

➤ _____

_____

_____

Mordecai's burlap sack and ashes told her a whole lot. Someone was dying or had died. And that's why Esther was distressed.

What did Esther do when she heard about Mordecai's condition?

➤ _____

_____

_____

There are lots of theories about why Esther sent Mordecai clothing. The one that makes the most sense to me is that she wanted to know why Mordecai was grieving, and she wanted to hear it from his own mouth. For that to happen, he had to come to the palace. And to enter the palace, you had to wear nice clothes, not burlap sacks and ashes.

But Mordecai would not change his clothes.

When Mordecai refused to put on the clothes Esther had sent him, she still wanted to know why her adoptive dad was mourning. So, she sent someone named Hathach to ask Mordecai what was wrong. And that's when Esther learned the reason for Mordecai's grieving.

OK, read Esther 4:5–9. Then, write down what Mordecai asks Esther to do.

➤ _____

_____

_____

Mordecai was asking Esther to do something really hard.

Do you think she wanted to go to King Xerxes and beg him to help her people? Circle one.

 yes ? no ?

Let's find out.

ESTHER 4:10-14

As you read the next part of the story, underline Esther's message back to Mordecai.

10 Then Esther told Hathach to go back and relay this message to Mordecai: 11 "All the king's officials and even the people in the provinces know that anyone who appears before the king in his inner court without being invited is doomed to die unless the king holds out his gold scepter. And the king has not called for me to come to him for thirty days." 12 So Hathach gave Esther's message to Mordecai. 13 Mordecai sent this reply to Esther: "Don't think for a moment that because you're in the palace you will escape when all other Jews are killed.

14 If you keep quiet at a time like this, deliverance and relief for the Jews will arise from some other place, but you and your relatives will die. Who knows if perhaps you were made queen for just such a time as this?"

Turn back to the page at the front of the book labeled "My Notes On Esther." It's finally time to write in some information about The Queen. Add her name and write down what you know about her.

Esther did **NOT** want to do what Mordecai requested. Why? Write the answer in your own words in the cartoon frame on the left.

Mordecai sends Esther another message in the cartoon frame in the middle. Tell what he said in your own words. (We'll come back to the cartoon frame on the right later.)

Mourning Mystery Mayhem

Esther basically asked Mordecai, "Are you **CRAZY**? I'll die!" But Mordecai was looking at the bigger picture. He could now see that God had placed Esther in a unique position and would be able to use her to help the Jews. And Mordecai is very sure God will use *someone* to help.

Fill in the blanks to rewrite Esther 4:14a below:

"If you keep _____ at a _____ like _____,

_____ and _____ for the Jews

_____ _____ from some other place."

FULL STOP! Why is Mordecai so confident? Time to **zoom out**!

ZOOM OUT!

Grab a gold or yellow pencil or marker. Read these verses and circle every time you read the name of the One who protects the Jewish people, who are also known as the nation of Israel.

> Indeed, he who watches over Israel never slumbers or sleeps. The LORD himself watches over you! The LORD stands beside you as your protective shade. The LORD keeps you from all harm and watches over your life. (Psalm 121:4–5, 7)

Psalm 121 is a great big promise from God to His special people, the Israelites. God promised to protect the Jews. And there are lots of verses like this in the Old Testament. **Mordecai must have known the Scriptures and believed them!**

Mordecai didn't tell Esther that she was their *only* hope. Instead, he said, "*God will not allow His people to be wiped out.*" But maybe this was why Esther had been chosen as queen **FOR SUCH A TIME AS THIS.** Maybe these circumstances were an invitation to her purpose in God's big plan.

ZOOM IN!

ESTHER 4:15-17

Let's see what Esther decides to do. After you read the verses below, go back to the third cartoon frame and write what Esther says in your own words.

15 Then Esther sent this reply to Mordecai: 16 "Go and gather together all the Jews of Susa and fast for me. Do not eat or drink for three days, night or day. My maids and I will do the same. And then, though it is against the law, I will go in to see the king. If I must die, I must die."

17 So Mordecai went away and did everything as Esther had ordered him.

When Esther finally had all the information, she basically said two things:

1 "Let's **ALL** fast and pray!"   **2** "I'm in. I'll do it!"

⟶ Esther fasted and prayed.

In the last chapter, we learned about *fasting*. Write the definition below.

⟹⟶ _____

_____

Remember, fasting without praying is not a fast at all. It's dieting. But Esther and all the rest of the Jewish people *were* praying. They were talking to God about their problem, and asking for His help.

Esther knew she needed wisdom from God to help her know how to talk to the king. *What should she say? How should she say it? When should she do it?*

By choosing to fast, Esther was admitting that she needed God. She could not carry out her purpose without Him.

⟶ Esther decided to do what she did not want to do.

Esther found the courage she needed to do what she did not want to do! That doesn't mean she wasn't still afraid. And it doesn't mean she was super excited to do what Mordecai asked her to do. It just means that she was choosing to trust God's plan for her life—even if it meant she might die. Sending that message to Mordecai was a declaration of great faith.

> IF I MUST DIE, I MUST DIE.

Go back to Esther 4:16 and underline Esther's words, "If I must die, I must die."

Those words show incredible faith in God. She recognizes that EVEN IF she dies, God will carry out His purpose.

So, did Esther march straight into the king's throne room to give him a piece of her mind about his decree? No! We'll study more about that in the next lesson. For now, let's zero in on what all of this means for you!

ZERO IN: What does it mean?

Did you know that **EVEN JESUS** had to do something He didn't want to do?

Jesus came to earth to die for our sins because it was the only way to keep sin from separating us from God. It was His purpose!

But when the time was near for Jesus to endure His terrible death on the cross, He pleaded with God:

 "Father, if you are willing, please take this cup of suffering away from me. Yet I want your will to be done, not mine." (Luke 22:42)

Underline the words that tell us Jesus didn't want to suffer. Then double underline the words that communicate He was still willing to die, even if He didn't want to.

Jesus was the Son of God. But He was also fully man! That means that He experienced this world in the same way that you and I do. He liked some things more than others. And one thing He didn't like was pain. He also had physical and emotional feelings just like you and me.

Circle the feelings below that you think Jesus might have felt when He prayed those words.

SAD   HAPPY

AFRAID

EXCITED   LONELY

We don't have to guess how He felt. This verse tells us.

Circle the word that reveals Jesus' emotions.

 He prayed more fervently, and he was in such agony of spirit that his sweat fell to the ground like great drops of blood. (Luke 22:44)

The Bible uses the word *agony* to describe how Jesus was feeling. That means he felt extreme physical or mental suffering at the thought of His death. This was so powerful that His sweat had blood in it.

And yet . . . Jesus said that He wanted God's will to be done. He was submitting to God's purpose for His life, even though it was hard and painful. Even though He was scared. *Even though He didn't want to!*

Jesus isn't the only one called to hard things, but He set a good example for us while He was here on earth. So did our girl, Esther. When she decided to do what she did not want to do and when she prayed and fasted.

Does it seem like a waste of time to pray and fast when we have an assignment from God? It's not! Praying and fasting give God an opportunity to get us ready to live out our purpose. Doing the important things He has planned for us requires preparation.

Let me remind you to talk to your mom if fasting is something you want to learn more about! It's important to do it wisely and safely and for the right reason—to pray and cry out to God. If there is something big and difficult going in your life, you could start learning to fast *with your mom* by skipping an afternoon snack and spending that time in prayer. But remember, your body is growing and you have to provide nutrients to it. You have to learn and train to fast with wisdom and help.

Think about when you play a sport. You don't jump right into the big championship game. First, you practice with your team. Then, you have regular season games where you slowly work your way up to the bigger championship games. The practices and regular season games aren't just something to keep you busy until the championships. They are preparing you! When God wants us to do something BIG, it requires SPIRITUAL preparation!

SPIRITUAL PRACTICE }

Find all the activities that help you get prepared to do what God asks you to do.

PRAYER   FASTING   READING THE WORD   WORSHIP   GODLY ADVICE

P R A Y E R X Q T S E B Y N E L A Y
C A K C R H U G B K T G Q R L L P D
W U H Q J E O N I Q T A H F Z R Q T
M E I L R V A R G C F Z U F Y I W E
R P M U Y O K D F N G H Q Y L D W B
Q U M D E Q Q O I P J Y I E C J O I
L U R R Y D D O R N E G K M R L R E
C M M A K O O J W R G S W N E I S M
V H T T E G K M Q K H T G A U F H S
W S E W Q K J G V D A K H M H T I I
D J K K C F H O O Z W R N E X L P V
I L N O R A X D J C E F A R W B U B
F R Q Q T R U L U W X N T M B O M K
S N C T D Q R Y G O N M K N P Y R O
X Z T V M Z I A F O Y H R R H V T D
U D G G N T Q D Q Q I O Q R C B E U
E O C L C C N V U R F Q C C B R J R
I D H I G Y D I P Q T R C O A X X L
F A S T I N G C L G E J U I F Y I Z
O Q B I P V O E B W X S P N Q S O I

*For puzzle answers, look in the back of the book.

We all have to do things we don't want to do sometimes. Usually, we don't want to do those things because we are worried we might lose something. Esther was worried she was going to lose her life. That's pretty intense. But we don't usually face that big of a loss.

But maybe there's something really BIG in your life right now that is requiring sacrifice. And you don't want to do it. Like maybe your dad just got a new job that seems like five million miles away from all of your friends and you have to move! That's a really big deal. God is calling your dad to move and his purpose is costing you something.

You can do what you don't want to do when you place your faith in God and believe that He will have new friendships or new experiences in a new place for you. Or you can grumble and complain and be even more miserable.

So, what's the thing in YOUR life, right now, that you just don't want to do?

➤ _____

_____

_____

Now, don't worry. It's not like God's up there saying, "Let me figure out what she most doesn't want to do!" That's not how it works. He loves you and wants you to enjoy your purpose. But sometimes, it does include doing things you don't understand just yet.

Let's zip this lesson up by talking to God about that!

ZIP IT UP: What does God want me to do with it?

We learned that Esther spent three days fasting and praying when she decided to do what she did not want to do. If there's something you need to do that you don't want to do, I encourage you to pray.

Do I encourage you to fast? At your age, I really think you need to have your mom help you decide if you're ready for that and it would be healthy for you to do it. If you both agree that you are, do something simple like skipping a snack or eating a super nutritional green smoothie for lunch instead of your favorite grilled cheese sandwich and tomato soup! And, of course, use that time to pray.

And, like Esther, ask others to pray with you.

I do want you to pray even if you don't fast. Let's start by writing a prayer to God asking for wisdom below. But then **TELL SOMEONE** about it and ask them to pray with you.

_____

_____

_____

_____

_____

Congratulations, True Girl! You just zoomed and zipped all through the capital of the Persian empire even though there's some major problems going on!

In the next lesson, we're going to find out what happens to Esther when she goes to see King Xerxes. **Will she live? Or will she die?**

✳ Nothing and No One Can Stop God's Purpose for Your Life

Way back in the 1920s, women were not really welcome to take lessons to fly airplanes. But Betty Greene wanted to so badly. She was only seven years old when Charles Lindbergh became the first pilot to fly all alone across the ocean, and it made her want to be a pilot too.

She had an older brother who did take flying lessons. He told Betty all about it and she would listen, hoping that she, too, could be a pilot someday.

But, many people had lost their jobs and homes. They couldn't even afford food, let alone things like flying lessons. This period was called the Great Depression.

There were a lot of things standing in the way, but Betty eventually achieved her dream. And she became the first pilot to fly for Missionary Aviation Fellowship, which is a group that flies planes for God's kingdom. Betty made over 4,640 flights and served the Lord in twelve different countries.[4]

It may have seemed to Betty like her dreams of being a pilot were gone forever when the Great Depression happened. But it was God's plan for her life to fly!

Welp. If you recall, a decree has been issued in Persia to wipe out God's special people, the Jews. (That's a big problem since the Jewish people were God's plan to bring the Savior into the world.) It might have seemed to Esther that all hope was gone. But don't worry! God's plan for her life was to be the Queen of Persia.

And for good reason, as we'll soon see!

Well, I know one thing for sure—SPOILER ALERT!—according to Daniel 6:15, the law of Persia stated that no edict or decree the king made could be changed. *King Xerxes could not reverse his command to wipe out the Jewish people if he wanted to.*

THE PLOT THICKENS! Will this be the end of God's purpose for the Jewish people?

Well, friend, it's time to do some **zooming**! But before we dive in, let's write the lessons we've learned so far. If you need help remembering, turn back to your Purpose Lessons page at the beginning of the book!

⭐ PURPOSE LESSON #1 _____

_____

⭐ PURPOSE LESSON #2 _____

_____

⭐ PURPOSE LESSON #3 _____

_____

⭐ PURPOSE LESSON #4 _____

_____

Good job! I'm going to share Purpose Lesson #5 later in this lesson. Let's start zooming.

Zoom In & Out—Who? What? Where? When? Why?

When Queen Esther went to King Xerxes to stand up for her people, she knew the risk: It was **ILLEGAL** to enter the king's court without an invitation. She could be killed on the spot!

What crazy courage this girl had!

BUT . . . Esther did something super important *before* she went in. Let's check it out.

ZOOM IN!

ESTHER 5:1-3

Read all of the passage below. What did Esther decide to wear when she made a surprise visit to King Xerxes? Use a fancy color like purple or gold to underline the answer.

1 On the third day of the fast, Esther put on her royal robes and entered

the inner court of the palace, just across from the king's hall. The king

was sitting on his royal throne, facing the entrance. *2* When he saw

Queen Esther standing there in the inner court, he welcomed her and

held out the gold scepter to her. So Esther approached and touched the end of the scepter.

3 Then the king asked her, "What do you want, Queen Esther? What is your request? I will give it

to you, even if it is half the kingdom!"

Esther put on her royal robes! Based on history books, we know this probably included elaborately embroidered robes plus an impressive array of jewelry. Her hair was likely braided with gold threads or ribbons. And . . . as queen . . . she topped it all off by wearing a royal headdress **OR CROWN**.

Esther did not show up to stand up for God in her spa lounging clothes!

Why? She was sending a message. She was communicating, "I am a woman of worth and dignity!" Her clothing reminded the king of her incredible position. Esther was **THE QUEEN OF PERSIA**!

She did not go to the king groveling, kneeling, or begging. She had learned through circumstances and wise counsel that God's big-picture plan was for her to be royalty. So, when it was time to fulfill her purpose, you better believe she wore her crown.

How did King Xerxes respond to **THE QUEEN OF PERSIA**?

Go back up to Esther 5:1–3 and draw a gold scepter above the words that describe the king's response to seeing his queen.

Do you remember from the last chapter why the king's response was such a big deal? In the book of Esther, chapter 4, Esther reminded Mordecai of a Persian law about the king's scepter. Unscramble the key words on the next page to reveal the law.

LAW LINGO } Unscramble the key words from Esther 4:11 to reveal the Persian law.

KEY WORDS

1. NIKG   2. CRTOU NNERI   3. TEDINVIT   4. IED   5. DOGL TERSCEPT

"All the king's officials and even the people in the provinces know that

anyone who appears before the 1. _____ _____ _____ _____ in his

2. _____ _____ _____ _____ _____   _____ _____ _____ _____ _____ without

being 3. _____ _____ _____ _____ _____ _____ _____ is doomed

to 4. _____ _____ _____ unless the king holds out his

5. _____ _____ _____ _____   _____ _____ _____ _____ _____ _____ _____ .

And the king has not called for me to come to him for thirty days."

* For puzzle answers, look in the back of the book.

The fact that King Xerxes held out his scepter to Queen Esther was **VERY** good news.

(Pssst! This is an example of God's *providence*! Do you remember that word from chapter 1? It is a word we use to describe the protective care of God. And it's going to become important in this lesson.)

So far, so good. The king was going to listen to Esther's request. And it seemed like he was feeling generous.

Based on Esther 5:3, what was King Xerxes willing to give to Esther?

ESTHER 5:4-8

Read the first verse below to find out what Esther requested from the king. Underline it.

4 And Esther replied, "If it please the king, let the king and Haman come today to a banquet I have prepared for the king." 5 The king turned to his attendants and said, "Tell Haman to come quickly to a banquet, as Esther has requested." So the king and Haman went to Esther's banquet. 6 And while they were drinking wine, the king said to Esther, "Now tell me what you really want. What is your request? I will give it to you, even if it is half the kingdom!"

7 Esther replied, "This is my request and deepest wish. 8 If I have found favor with the king, and if it pleases the king to grant my request and do what I ask, please come with Haman tomorrow to the banquet I will prepare for you. Then I will explain what this is all about."

Of course, the king says, "Yes." And then he asks her, "Now, what do you really want?" Read verses 5–8 above to see what Esther asks for at that banquet. Double underline it!

Now what happens next is the stuff *providence* is made of!

Picture this: Haman was walking home after the banquet. Actually, he was probably strutting like the man of importance he thought he was. I can imagine him swishing his robes, chin high in the air. And then he saw Mordecai by the king's gate doing his job well—making sure nobody got in who wasn't supposed to be there. But there was one thing he didn't do: bow down before Haman.

Haman was furious! He must have thought, *I can't wait a whole year to get rid of this Mordecai guy on the day we kill all the Jews! I've got to do it NOW!* His wife and friends helped him make an evil plan to kill Mordecai in a horrible way. All Haman needed was the king's approval, which he planned to get after a good night of sleep.

But there was someone who wasn't getting a good night of sleep: the king. He couldn't fall asleep so decided he needed a bedtime story. He asked a servant to bring the Book of Annals, which contained the history of everything he had done as king. And the servant read something like this:

ESTHER 2:21-23

21 One day as Mordecai was on duty at the king's gate, two of the king's eunuchs, Bigthana and Teresh—who were guards at the door of the king's private quarters—became angry at King Xerxes and plotted to assassinate him. 22 But Mordecai heard about the plot and gave the information to Queen Esther. She then told the king about it and gave Mordecai credit for the report. 23 When an investigation was made and Mordecai's story was found to be true, the two men were impaled on a sharpened pole. This was all recorded in *The Book of the History of King Xerxes' Reign.*

The king realized, as the servant was reading, that he had forgotten to reward Mordecai for saving him. And that is the exact moment Haman walked into the king's chamber. Esther 6:6 records how the conversation went.

"Hey, Haman!" the king said as soon as he walked in. "What should I do to honor a man who truly pleases me?"

Haman thought that *he* must be the man the king wanted to honor so he listed off a whole slew of ridiculously glamorous things to do. We find them in Esther 6:7–9.

Turn back to the page at the front of the book labeled "My Notes On Esther." Write in some information about Haman. He's "The Bad Guy." Add his name and write down what you know about him.

HAMAN'S DREAM }

Decode the message below to find out what Haman was dreaming would be *his* reward. (But it was really for Mordecai!) Each letter in the phrase has been replaced with a random letter or number. Try to decode the message.

A	B	C	D	E	F	G	H	I	J	K	L	M	N	O	P	Q	R	S	T	U	V	W	X	Y	Z
5							20	2		4		26		16		7									

```
        _  I  _  _        H  I  M     A  _  R  O  _  A        R  O  _  _
       19  2 13  3       20  2 26     5  7 16 12  5 22        7 16 25  3

    A  _  _     _  _  _        H  I  M        O  R  R  O        _  H  _
    5 23  9    22  3 15       20  2 26       25 16  7  7 16  1     15 20  3

  K  I  _  _  _        H  O  R  _     .     A  R  A  _  _        H  I  M
  4  2 23 19 17       20 16  7 17  3       14  5  7  5  9  3       20  2 26

        A  R  O  _  _  _        O  _  _  _        O  R  _
        5  7 16 21 23  9       15 16  1 23       11 16  7

              _  _  _  R  _  O  _  _  _        O  _        O  _  _  _  .
              3 13  3  7 12 16 23  3          15 16       17  3  3
```

* For puzzle answers, look in the back of the book.

Can you imagine the sucker punch to the gut when the king told Haman, "Wow! What an excellent idea! Go do all of that for Mordecai."

OK, so big question: Do you think it "just so happened" that the king was reminded to reward Mordecai on the very day Haman wanted to kill him? Circle one.

yep, it was an amazing coincidence.

Nope, that was God's providence at work for sure.

I don't know.

I believe it was the miraculous protective care of God.

And it set Esther up for the second banquet she was going to host for King Xerxes and Haman that very night!

When Haman walked into Esther's banquet that night, he was no longer swishing his robes and his chin was no longer held high. He may have tried to force a smile and pretend like nothing was wrong. But his day was about to get even worse. Because this was the moment Esther had chosen to reveal the truth.

She told the king EVERYTHING: How a decree had been passed to kill her people and how Haman was the man behind it. Then, to add fuel to the fire, one of the king's servants told him that Haman had been planning to kill Mordecai in a really terrible way. That sealed the deal and the king commanded: "Go kill Haman in that very same way!"

The bad guy lost and now Esther's people were safe and everyone lived happily ever after, right? WRONG! There was still one super bad ginormous problem!

ESTHER 8:1-6

Read the verses below. When you get to verse 8, double underline Esther's request.

1 On that same day King Xerxes gave the property of Haman, the enemy of the Jews, to Queen Esther. Then Mordecai was brought before the king, for Esther had told the king how they were related.

2 The king took off his signet ring—which he had taken back from Haman—and gave it to Mordecai. And Esther appointed Mordecai to be in charge of Haman's property. 3 Then Esther went again before the king, falling down at his feet and begging him with tears to stop the evil plot devised by Haman the Agagite against the Jews. 4 Again the king held out the gold scepter to Esther. So she rose and stood before him. 5 Esther said, "If it please the king, and if I have found favor with him, and if he thinks it is right, and if I am pleasing to him, let there be a decree that reverses the orders of Haman son of Hammedatha the Agagite, who ordered that Jews throughout all the king's provinces should be destroyed. 6 For how can I endure to see my people and my family slaughtered and destroyed?"

Even though evil Haman was dead,
the decree to kill all of the Jews was still in place.

 THE PUZZLE PIECES OF ESTHER'S PROBLEM } On the left side are some important verses we have studied. Match them to the facts on the right side.

There were many people in Susa who did not like these people (Esther 2:10)

A rule or decree from the king of Persia

Esther's friends and family would be killed on this day (Esther 3:7)

The Jews or Israelites

It could never be changed (Daniel 6:12)

March 7th of the next year

* For puzzle answers, look in the back of the book.

 ESTHER 8:7-13

Don't worry! God had caused the king to really like Esther and Mordecai. Even though he could not change his decree, he had a good idea. Read about it below. Underline verse 11.

7 Then King Xerxes said to Queen Esther and Mordecai the Jew . . .

8 "Now go ahead and send a message to the Jews in the king's name, telling them whatever you want, and seal it with the king's signet ring. But remember that whatever has already been written in the king's name and sealed with his signet ring can never be revoked." 9 . . . [A] decree was written in the scripts and languages of all the people of the empire, including that of the Jews. 10 The decree

was written in the name of King Xerxes and sealed with the king's signet ring. Mordecai sent

the dispatches by swift messengers, who rode fast horses especially for the king's service.

11 The king's decree gave the Jews in every city authority to unite to defend their lives. They were

allowed to kill, slaughter, and annihilate anyone of any nationality or province who might attack

them or their children and wives, and to take the property of their enemies. 12 The day chosen

for this event throughout all the provinces of King Xerxes was March 7 of the next year. 13 A copy

of this decree was to be issued as law in every province and proclaimed to all peoples, so that

the Jews would be ready to take revenge on their enemies on the appointed day.

Write below what the new decree allowed the Jews to do.

_____

_____

_____

Mordecai was a wise man and he knew what to do. He had the king's secretaries write a new decree that said this: THE JEWS COULD FIGHT BACK!

If you're like me, you don't like the verses in the Bible that describe war and death. But what we're reading about in the book of Esther is about the Jewish people defending themselves. If they did not, they would be killed. And doing this was the only way to PROTECT and PRESERVE God's people. The decree Mordecai wrote didn't allow the Jewish people to kill just anyone. They were only allowed to defend themselves, protecting their families.

The king sent his men on his fastest horses to get the word out to all 127 provinces. That was a big area to cover!

Let's look at our map at the beginning of the book again. Can you draw a path for the horses from Susa to each area of the map?

Whew! That was a close call! Of course, it's not over. The next chapter of Esther describes the massive battle that took place. Those who were hoping to overpower the Jews had a big surprise coming! All over the land, the Jews struck down their enemies. Many people lost their lives, but the Jews had the victory and God's people were saved! For so much of Esther's story, it looked like there was no way to save the Jews.

But here comes **PURPOSE LESSON #5:**
NOTHING and NO ONE can stop God's purpose for your life.

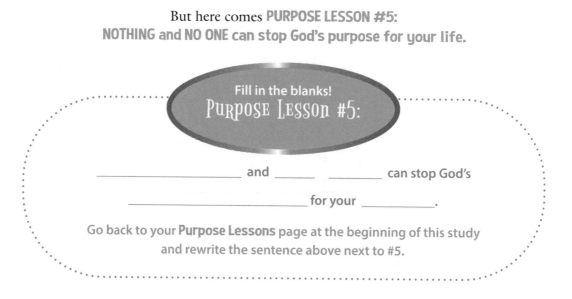

Fill in the blanks!
PURPOSE LESSON #5:

_____ and _____ _____ can stop God's

_____ for your _____.

Go back to your **Purpose Lessons** page at the beginning of this study and rewrite the sentence above next to #5.

God's power is **ALWAYS** enough to overcome any problem.

 ZERO IN: What does it mean?

Circle the three things in the verse below that cannot stand against God's plan.

No human wisdom or understanding or plan can stand against the LORD. (Proverbs 21:30)

Does this mean that nothing bad will ever happen? Of course not. Bad things will still happen in your life. But you don't have to be afraid. Even when you cannot see God,

He is still taking care of you. That's how *providence* works, remember?

Now, that doesn't mean you just sit back and let anything happen. Esther and Mordecai took action. And I want to zero in on one important part of that today.

When Esther went to the king, she wore her crown and royal robe. Why? Because she knew her position as the queen of Persia. Esther was seated on the throne of Persia. If you call yourself a Christian, you, too, have a position. And you must never forget it.

Read the verse below and circle where YOU are seated.

 For he raised us from the dead along with Christ and seated us with him in the heavenly realms because we are united with Christ Jesus. (Ephesians 2:6)

You are seated *with Jesus*! That's incredible news. When you are a Christian, you are adopted into God's family. And Jesus is the King of kings.

What do you call the adopted daughter of a king?

_____

Being adopted into God's family makes you a princess! Like Esther, you get to dress the part. But instead of jewels and a crown, Jesus clothes you in righteousness, which is a lot like a spiritual crown.

When we are in trouble, we've got to find ways to remember what our position is. One way to remember is by reading the Bible. And it might help you remember even more if you sing about what the Bible says! True Girl has a song that can help with that. It's called **Wear My Crown**. Check out the words of the chorus:

I am a royal---Jesus, You say I'm enough
I love to know that I am worthy of your love
I know who I am---You're my inheritance
I'm clothed in beauty---now I will wear my crown[5]

You can get all our True Girl albums at mytruegirl.com. Some songs are available wherever you like to stream music.

These words are based on the Truth that you are the daughter of a king! Even princesses can feel discouraged, but Jesus wants you to know and believe that He has your back. And even more importantly, *He has a plan*!

I think we need to zip it up with some prayer and ask God to grow your faith and remind you who He made you to be.

ZIP IT UP: What does God want me to do with it?

OK, you might be thinking, *but what about when those bad things are happening? How am I supposed to know that God is going to work everything out?*

That, my friend, is called FAITH. And the Bible says that faith comes from hearing the words of the Bible (Romans 10:17). I think that's how Mordecai was able to be so full of faith. He knew the words of God recorded in Scripture and so he believed "deliverance will come" (Esther 4:14).

When you're in a tough situation, you can practice faith by reminding yourself of the Truth found in the Bible.

Think of some of the things you are worried about right now and write about them in the blanks below. Like, "If my dad loses his job" or "If I don't make the soccer team."

If _____,

God will be with me.

If _____,

God will take care of me.

If _____,

God still has a plan.

If _____,

God's plan can never be thwarted.

Once you fill in the blanks, read those sentences out loud. Do you believe the words you're saying? Or do you still have doubts?

Pray right now, telling God what you're thinking. Ask Him to help you grow your faith so that you can walk in confidence that He is with you and will **ALWAYS** help you live out your purpose. You could even write your prayer in the space below if you want.

CHAPTER 6

✳ God's Purpose Is Worth Celebrating!

Let's say I invite you to come visit my hobby farm for a big party. I want to introduce you to Boo Who, my favorite mini-silkie fainting goat, and together we will gather tail feathers from Bonaparte, my magnificent black-shouldered peacock. Then, we'll have a barbecue to celebrate something very special.

There's just one problem! You've never been to my farm before.

I text your mom the best directions. My farm is tucked in a little hollow not far from town, but it's not that easy to find if you don't know how to get there. Sometimes, the GPS doesn't work. So, my directions include special landmarks like the traffic light on Benner Pike, the bubbling creek you'll drive by, the freaky underpass you'll drive below, and the name of my little gravel lane.

The directions end with, "Drive all the way to the big round riding ring at the end of the lane. That's our farm!" You eventually pull in. I'm there, waiting with my horses Trigg and Truett saddled so we can go for a quick ride.

The next time you come, though, I'll be with you. (We'll meet at Sweet Frog for *fro-yo* before you come.) You won't need directions. I'll be your map. All you have to do is listen to me and follow my directions. Turn by turn, we'll find our way back to the big, round riding ring.

Which sounds easier?

Yeah, it sounds a lot more relaxing and restful for me to be in the car with you, right?

Well, what if I told you . . . we need to live like that!

Jesus . . . is right beside you . . . telling you where to go.

Rest in that!

But, party too! Because there is purpose in parties. And there are plenty of parties to learn from in the book of Esther! But before we get to that, let's review what we've covered so far. Remember, you've already written all of the purpose lessons at the beginning of this book. So feel free to turn back to that page if you need help!

⭐ **PURPOSE LESSON #1** _____

_____

⭐ **PURPOSE LESSON #2** _____

_____

⭐ **PURPOSE LESSON #3** _____

_____

⭐ **PURPOSE LESSON #4** _____

_____

⭐ **PURPOSE LESSON #5** _____

_____

I'm going to need a drumroll as we introduce our **LAST** purpose lesson!

PURPOSE LESSON #6: God's purpose is worth celebrating!

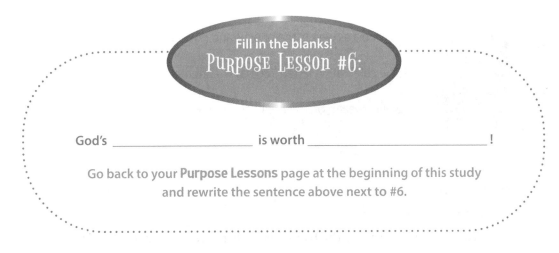

Fill in the blanks!

PURPOSE LESSON #6:

God's _____ is worth _____!

Go back to your **Purpose Lessons** page at the beginning of this study and rewrite the sentence above next to #6.

Esther's journey wasn't always easy. And yours might not be either. But when you're following God's purpose for your life, there is always reason to celebrate. After all, Jesus has already won the battle between good and evil! Let's talk about the purpose in parties.

The story of Esther **BEGAN** with a party where King Xerxes was made famous. The story **HINGED** on two parties thrown by Esther to carry out God's plan. And the story **RESULTS** in a party. Let's learn more.

I think it's time to zoom in one last time. (You might want to grab your party hat!)

Zoom In & Out—Who? What? Where? When? Why?

ZOOM IN!

Do you remember the very first party in the book of Esther?

Let me further jog your memory with the description of this party straight from chapter 1 of Esther. On the next page, underline what King Xerxes was displaying.

ESTHER 1:3-4

3 In the third year of his reign, [King Xerxes] gave a banquet for all his nobles and officials. He invited all the military officers of Persia and Media as well as the princes and nobles of the provinces.

4 The celebration lasted 180 days—a tremendous display of the opulent wealth of his empire and the pomp and splendor of his majesty.

King Xerxes' party had a purpose: **to show off his riches and glory.** He planned the celebration to make himself famous.

In the last chapter, we studied the banquets Esther threw to talk to the king about the **SUPER BIG PROBLEM.** Those parties had a purpose: **to rescue God's people who were part of God's BIG PICTURE plan to send Jesus to us.**

And now, we're to the end of Esther! Let's see how the story ends. (Hint: It's a party!)

ESTHER 8:16-17

Read the verses below and draw happy faces above the emotions the Jews were feeling.

16 The Jews were filled with joy and gladness and were honored everywhere. 17 In every province and city, wherever the king's decree arrived, the Jews rejoiced and had a great celebration and declared a public festival and holiday. And many of the people of the land became Jews themselves, for they feared what the Jews might do to them.

Go back through the verses and circle what the Jews decided to do to express their joy and gladness.

ESTHER 9:20-24, 26-31

The celebration the Jews decided to have was so big, it had a name. Underline the name of this final party in the book of Esther as you read!

20 Mordecai recorded these events and sent letters to the Jews near and far, throughout all the provinces of King Xerxes, 21 calling on them to celebrate an annual festival on these two days. 22 He told them to celebrate these days with feasting and gladness and by giving gifts of food to each other and presents to the poor. This would commemorate a time when the Jews gained relief from their enemies, when their sorrow was turned into gladness and their mourning into joy. 23 So the Jews accepted Mordecai's proposal and adopted this annual custom. 24 Haman son of Hammedatha the Agagite, the enemy of the Jews, had plotted to

crush and destroy them on the date determined by casting lots (the lots were called *purim*). . . .

26 That is why this celebration is called Purim, because it is the ancient word for casting lots.

So because of Mordecai's letter and because of what they had experienced, 27 the Jews

throughout the realm agreed to inaugurate this tradition and to pass it on to their descendants

and to all who became Jews. They declared they would never fail to celebrate these two

prescribed days at the appointed time each year. 28 These days would be remembered and

kept from generation to generation and celebrated by every family throughout the provinces

and cities of the empire. This Festival of Purim would never cease to be celebrated among the

Jews, nor would the memory of what happened ever die out among their descendants.

29 Then Queen Esther, the daughter of Abihail, along with Mordecai the Jew, wrote another

letter putting the queen's full authority behind Mordecai's letter to establish the Festival of Purim.

30 Letters wishing peace and security were sent to the Jews throughout the 127 provinces of

the empire of Xerxes. 31 These letters established the Feast of Purim—an annual celebration

of these days at the appointed time, decreed by both Mordecai the Jew and Queen Esther.

(The people decided to observe this festival, just as they had decided for themselves and their

descendants to establish the times of fasting and mourning.)

The Festival of Purim is still celebrated today! Look at verse 24 and explain below where the name came from.

Verse 28 tells us the Festival of Purim was not going to be celebrated just once.

Write how long it would be celebrated below.

The Festival of Purim was so very different from the party King Xerxes threw in the beginning of our story. And it's also different from the banquets Esther threw for King Xerxes and Haman. But before you can understand why, you have to understand a little bit about ownership.

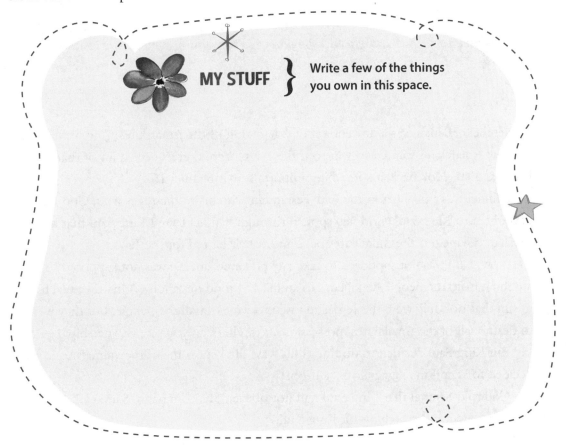

MY STUFF } Write a few of the things you own in this space.

What does that have to do with King Xerxes and Esther and parties?

Well, we already know that King Xerxes threw a big shindig to make himself famous. But more than that, he was claiming ownership of his kingdom. He was saying, "Look at all of these riches and beautiful things that are **ALL MINE!**"

Purim was radically different. Look at verse 22 and write below two specific things Mordecai told the Jews to do to celebrate Purim.

Instead of claiming ownership, the Jewish people were **GIVING UP** ownership to make God famous. They had just experienced a great victory over their enemies, but instead of celebrating their power and taking things from their enemies, they celebrated by *giving* gifts to the poor.

Hold on a sec! Time to zoom out! We just read something super important!

ZOOM OUT!

Remember: Haman was a descendant of Agag, king of the Amalekites. And we learned that the Amalekites wanted to wipe out the Jews. (Yep, there's been a lot of that in history.) Let's look back at something important in 1 Samuel 15.

Samuel was a prophet in the Old Testament who heard messages from God and gave them to King Saul. God had spoken through Samuel to tell King Saul that he needed to wipe out the Amalekites because of their hatred for the Jews.

Now, Saul was not supposed to take any prisoners and he was not supposed to take anything from the people he killed. No animals or food or candles or hardware. That meant that not only were the Jews supposed to wipe out all the people, but they were to destroy all of the Amalekites' possessions, as well. (Can you say, "ownership"?)

But King Saul decided to do things his way. He kept some of the animals. And Saul decided to keep King Agag alive. (Uh-oh!)

God told Samuel that King Saul had not obeyed His command. Samuel was pretty upset and went out searching for King Saul.

 When Samuel finally found him, Saul greeted him cheerfully, "May the LORD bless you," he said. "I have carried out the LORD's command!"
"Then what is all the bleating of sheep and goats and the lowing of cattle I hear?" Samuel demanded. "It's true that the army spared the best of the sheep, goats, and cattle," Saul admitted. "But they are going

to sacrifice them to the LORD your God. We have destroyed everything else." Then Samuel said to Saul, "Stop! Listen to what the LORD told me last night!" "What did he tell you?" Saul asked. And Samuel told him, "Although you may think little of yourself, are you not the leader of the tribes of Israel? The LORD has anointed you king of Israel. And the LORD sent you on a mission and told you, 'Go and completely destroy the sinners, the Amalekites, until they are all dead.' Why haven't you obeyed the LORD? Why did you rush for the plunder and do what was evil in the LORD's sight?" "But I did obey the LORD," Saul insisted. "I carried out the mission he gave me. I brought back King Agag, but I destroyed everyone else. Then my troops brought in the best of the sheep, goats, cattle, and plunder to sacrifice to the LORD your God in Gilgal." But Samuel replied, "What is more pleasing to the LORD: your burnt offerings and sacrifices or your obedience to his voice? Listen! Obedience is better than sacrifice, and submission is better than offering the fat of rams." (1 Samuel 15:13–22)

God had called King Saul to fight to protect His people. The Amalekites were enemies of God's holy people and were fighting against (or discouraging) God's purpose. When God commanded King Saul to wipe them out, the purpose was NOT to increase the wealth of the Jews by allowing them to take ownership of the things that others once owned. The purpose was to protect God's plan to bring a Savior, Jesus Christ, into the world through the Jewish people.

OK, let's zoom on back to Esther's time.

ZOOM IN!

Esther and her people would have known about the war between King Saul and the Amalekites. And they would have known about Saul's disobedience when he took plunder and left King Agag alive. When Mordecai wrote the decree allowing the Jews to defend themselves, it was written that the Jews were also permitted to take things from their enemies. But the people chose not to do that. It's very possible that the people viewed this as a correction of the battle between King Saul and the Amalekites many years before.

Once the battle was completed, they celebrated with the Festival of Purim. The purpose of THIS party was to celebrate God's *providence*.

There's something I want you to take notice of: the Jews did not celebrate the anniversary of the battle. They celebrated the anniversary of the day after the battle—the day of their rest. This choice is a good reminder that we can rest in God's providence. We can trust Him to bring us through the battle to our day of rest.

ZERO IN: What does it mean?

It's important to take time to rest and celebrate God's providence. We need to learn from Purim. You and I can rest in God's provision.

In the space below, write some ways God has provided for you or your family. Then write some ideas about how you can rest.

God's plan is to eventually stop **ALL** death **FOREVER**. And He tells us about that plan in the Bible! Underline the plan as you read the verse below.

> God has now revealed to us his mysterious will regarding Christ—
> which is to fulfill his own good plan. And this is the plan: At the
> right time he will bring everything together under the authority of
> Christ—everything in heaven and on earth. (Ephesians 1:9–10)

Esther was a part of that plan! She played an important part in saving the Jews so that Jesus could be sent to earth. Now that Jesus has come, we **ALSO** play a part in His plan!

★ ★ ★

 GUESS what?! I have a little gift for you!

It's a coloring page that shows one way Jewish people celebrate Purim. Do you see the dotted line? **I want you to take some scissors and cut that page out— yes, you heard me right—CUT it OUt!** After you've cut it out, take pens, pencils, markers, or paint and color, **color**, **color**! Hang it up somewhere in your home to help you remember God's providence and faithfulness.

ZIP IT UP: What does God want me to do with it?

Even though God's plan hasn't come to full completion, there is still reason to celebrate! How have **YOU** seen God work in your life? If you can't think of anything, ask your mom or an older woman you trust how **THEY** have seen God work in their life. God's provision every day is something worth celebrating.

The reason that Esther planned a party that is still celebrated to this day is because it is good to **REMEMBER** God's providence and faithfulness. Many of our traditions and celebrations enable us to do this. For example:

 Christmas helps us remember the birth of Jesus.

Easter helps us remember the death and resurrection of Jesus.

Ascension Day helps us remember the day Jesus went up to heaven in the clouds.

And Purim helps us remember God's deliverance.

Every time you celebrate one of these special events, they're not just eating festive food or having fun. They're for **REMEMBERING** God's providence and faithfulness to us.

Today, as you zip it up, I want to invite you to **CELEBRATE**! You can throw a party just like Esther and her people did. Or bake some yummy Purim cookies. Or you can just draw some fun pictures of how the Jews **REMEMBER** God's faithful deliverance. I've included some information about Purim on the following page to give you some ideas!

PURIM: A PARTY WITH A PURPOSE

Purim is the Jewish holiday that celebrates God's rescue of His people in ancient Persia. You might want to have a Purim Party to celebrate your completion of the study of Esther, or at least bake some tasty Hamantaschen cookies.

Here are some fun ways Jewish people like to celebrate Purim:

Dress up in costumes
This is one of the most popular Purim traditions! You can make up fun costumes from things you have at home. Or make some puppets.

Plan a Purim meal
The Book of Esther has lots of banquets. The cookies are supposed to symbolize Haman's pockets or ears, depending on who you ask.

Make noisemakers
Somewhere along the way, it became popular to make noise to celebrate Purim.

Create Purim gift baskets
Early Jews are said to have shared their banquets with people who could not otherwise afford delicious feasts. Today, some people make food baskets to share with people in need.

DRAW SOME fun pictures of Purim!

Hamantaschen Cookie Recipe

INGREDIENTS

1 stick butter or margarine
1 egg
1 cup sugar
1 tsp. vanilla
2 Tbsps. orange juice
2 cups flour
2 tsps. baking powder
Salt, pinch
Any flavor pastry or pie filling

DIRECTIONS

1. Preheat your oven to 375 degrees.
2. Mix together margarine, egg, sugar, vanilla, and orange juice.
3. Add flour, baking powder, and salt. Mix well.
4. Roll out the dough on a floured board to 1/4-inch thickness. Cut into circles. Fill the circles with pastry filling and pinch dough into triangles around the filling. Place on a cookie sheet.
5. Bake at 375 degrees for 15 to 20 minutes until lightly browned.

YUM! YUM! YUM! YUM! YUM! YUM!

How Do I Become a Christian?[6]

I'm glad you asked. God loves us so much He sent His Son Jesus to die on the cross for us. Though you might actually know this Bible verse by memory, I want you to read it one more time. It's an important one!

 "For this is how God loved the world: He gave his one and only Son, so that everyone who believes in him will not perish but will have eternal life." (John 3:16)

Why did Jesus die for us? He died because of our sin.

When we disobey God or choose to do wrong, we sin. Things like being mean, lying, or cheating are examples of sin. The Bible says that every single human who ever walked the earth has sinned. That includes you and me.

Sin separates us from God. And the Bible says the punishment for sin is death. **BUT GOD LOVES US**, so He sent His Son Jesus to die on a cross. The great news is that Jesus didn't stay dead. He came back to life with the power to forgive our sins. And, He offers us the free gift of His salvation.

I don't know about you, but I've never gotten a free gift without having to reach out to accept it. You accept God's free gift of salvation by *believing* in Jesus and *receiving* Him as your Savior.

To **believe** in Jesus means:

♥ to trust Jesus

♥ to know Jesus is God's Son

♥ to know Jesus saves you from your sin

♥ to be willing to give Jesus control of your life

Do you believe in Jesus?

If so, you are ready to *receive* Jesus as your Savior, which means you ask Jesus to live inside of you and be in charge of your life. Romans 10:9 reads, "If you openly declare that Jesus is Lord and believe in your heart that God raised him from the dead, you will be saved."

Have you ever received Jesus by asking Him to forgive you of your sins?

If not, would you pray this prayer now?

Dear Lord, I admit to You that I am a sinner.

I thank You for sending Jesus to die on the cross for my sins.

I ask You to forgive me of my sins. I invite You to come into my life

to be my Lord. Thank You for saving me.

In Jesus' name, Amen.

Did you just pray that prayer for the first time?

If so, write the date below.

 The date I became a Christian:

_____

Congratulations!

Now, be sure to tell someone like your mom or your pastor.

They're going to be so excited!

WELCOME TO TRUE GIRL BIBLE STUDY

Mom's or Small Group Leader's Guide
for a Six- or Seven-Week Experience[7]

ere's how you can lead your daughter or a small group through this study: You can do it daily in a camp-style setting, or a much more digestible schedule is to tackle one chapter a week. If you're doing your first True Girl Bible study, you'll need seven weeks so you can cover the "How to Study the Bible" section during the first week. If you're a True Girl Bible study veteran, you could opt to skip the "How to Study the Bible" section and just jump right into chapter 1! In that case, you'll only need six weeks.

God will guide you in the best way to approach your discussion time, but here's what I'd suggest:

1. Get your own copy of this book and do the homework at the same pace as your daughter or small group. To be effective, you need your own copy of the book so you can study along. When I teach one of my own Bible studies online, I also do the homework in real time so that my heart is in tune with what God wants me to learn. In doing so, I'm emotionally and spiritually prepared to guide others through the content. It is challenging to be led by the Spirit and lead others if you're not engaged with God's Word in the same intimate way they have been. So, dive right on in together!

2. Select two key conversation questions from each chapter. One question can be from a core passage of Scripture in the *Zoom In & Out* section. This will help you discern what they've grappled with mentally in their studies. The second question can be from the *Zero In* section. This will help them verbalize and share where they need practical and emotional help. Just have fun gabbing about God's Word (and maybe include your favorite snack or dessert)!

3. Pray with your daughter or small group. Based on what they share each week, spend some time praying together. I also encourage you to pray for them throughout the week—in doing so, you'll have the privilege of seeing greater fruit. Pray for their heart to be open, softened, and receptive.

Encouraging Bible study for older users. For girls ages 10–12, this book is a challenge, but very age appropriate. For far too long, we have been expecting far too little of children when they study their Bibles. While I hope this is a fun experience with puzzles and interactivity, my goal is for them to get a taste of how wonderful it is to work diligently toward understanding and applying God's Word. Over and over, I'm asked how to make something easier for a tween or a teen. But let me encourage you: Why not try letting them jump into the deep end and experience the thrill!? If they need a life-preserver, send them one, but you might be surprised how well they can swim in the deep end of Scripture.

Simplifying the study for younger users. For girls ages 7–9, look for the flower icon.

Each time they reach this, it's time to stop! These icons divide chapters 1–6 into two parts, making one day's worth of homework time shorter and easier to digest. This means that younger girls can schedule two homework sessions each week instead of one so that they finish the chapter at the same time as older girls would. Ultimately, *you* know what's best and can curate the best study plan for your girl(s).

Dannah Gresh
Founder, True Girl

ANSWERS TO PUZZLES

Answer to *"The Purpose of the Party"* on page 29:

R	K	C	J	I	V	F	N	O	L	
M	I	O	L	I	Q	U	O	W	F	
A	D	U	P	W	E	A	L	T	H	
J	F	J	O	C	E	W	C	X	L	
E	L	Z	M	M	M	X	N	B	K	
S	W	W	P	P	F	J	H	B	W	
T	S	P	L	E	N	D	O	R	H	
Y	F	N	U	R	C	R	I	Y	T	
Y	W	X	X	F	T	H	C	X	M	
N	E	D	J	A	M	F	K	T	W	

Answer to *"Mordecai's Heart"* on page 51:

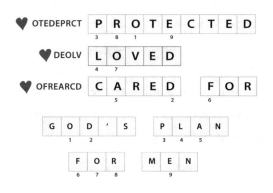

♥ OTEDEPRCT P R O T E C T E D
 3 8 1 9

♥ DEOLV L O V E D
 4 7

♥ OFREARCD C A R E D F O R
 5 2 6

G O D ' S P L A N
1 2 3 4 5

F O R M E N
6 7 8 9

Answer to *"Boys vs. Girls"* on page 35:

Answer to *"Find the Enemies of the Jewish People"* on page 64:

D	A	J	P	S	H	U	A	Z	F	W	V	E	A	Y
D	C	W	A	H	V	J	P	F	D	C	O	T	S	B
R	J	A	O	B	I	U	D	F	B	F	S	K	S	V
A	H	X	N	R	X	L	J	L	Z	V	O	H	Y	J
M	M	R	S	A	O	M	I	K	T	F	P	A	R	G
A	T	W	J	L	A	Y	G	S	S	P	N	V	I	Q
L	D	Q	V	L	Z	N	T	Q	T	D	F	C	A	D
E	I	K	L	U	T	K	I	Q	J	I	X	T	N	G
K	D	B	R	D	L	U	Z	T	N	I	N	U	S	G
I	F	R	X	N	Q	E	S	G	E	H	Y	E	H	Z
T	X	T	I	U	V	R	C	W	R	S	J	K	S	A
E	W	K	T	V	Z	K	I	I	E	O	A	J	V	S
S	M	B	A	B	Y	L	O	N	I	A	N	S	B	K
W	X	V	U	Q	L	J	A	H	K	E	I	V	M	Q
A	B	J	K	I	D	F	B	E	Q	G	F	F	N	F

Answer to *"Discouraging Discourse"* on page 69:

Answer to *"The Star of Our Story"* on page 47:

Answer to *"Spiritual Practice"* on page 89:

```
P R A Y E R X Q T S E B Y N E L A Y
C A K C R H U G B K T G Q R L L P D
W U H Q J E O N I Q T A H F Z R Q T
M E I L R V A R G C F Z U F Y I W E
R P M U Y O K D F N G H Q Y L D W B
Q U M D E Q Q O I P J Y I E C J O I
L U R R Y D D O R N E G K M R L R E
C M M A K O O J W R G S W N E I S M
V H T T E G K M Q K H T G A U F H S
W S E W Q K J G V D A K H M H T I I
D J K K C F H O O Z W R N E X L P V
I L N O R A X D J C E F A R W B U B
F R Q Q T R U L U W X N T M B O M K
S N C T D Q R Y G O N M K N P Y R O
X Z T V M Z I A F O Y H R R H V T D
U D G G N T Q D Q Q I O Q R C B E U
E O C L C C N V U R F Q C C B R J R
I D H I G Y D I P Q T R C O A X X L
F A S T I N G C L G E J U I F Y I Z
O Q B I P V O E B W X S P N Q S O I
```

Answer to "The Puzzle Pieces of *Esther's Problem*" on page 102:

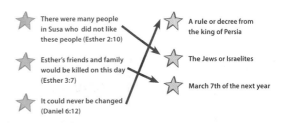

There were many people in Susa who did not like these people (Esther 2:10)

Esther's friends and family would be killed on this day (Esther 3:7)

It could never be changed (Daniel 6:12)

A rule or decree from the king of Persia

The Jews or Israelites

March 7th of the next year

Answer to *"Law Lingo"* on page 97:

"All the king's officials and even the people in the provinces know that anyone who appears before the 1. **K I N G** in his 2. **I N N E R   C O U R T** without being 3. **I N V I T E D** is doomed to 4. **D I E** unless the king holds out his 5. **G O L D   S C E P T E R**

And the king has not called for me to come to him for thirty days."

Answer to *"Haman's Dream"* on page 100:

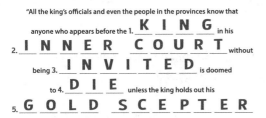

G I V E   H I M   A   R O Y A L   R O B E
19 2 13 3   20 2 26   5   7 16 12 5 22   7 16 25 3

A N D   L E T   H I M   B O R R O W   T H E
5 23 9   22 3 15   20 2 26   25 16 7 7 16 1   15 20 3

K I N G 'S   H O R S E .   P A R A D E   H I M
4 2 23 19 17   20 16 7 17 3   14 5 7 5 9 3   20 2 26

A R O U N D   T O W N   F O R
5 7 16 21 23 9   15 16 1 23   11 16 7

E V E R Y O N E   T O   S E E .
3 13 3 7 12 16 23 3   15 16   17 3 3

NOTES

1. This introduction is adapted from Dannah Gresh, *Ruth: Becoming a Girl of Loyalty* (Chicago: Moody Publishers, 2021).

2. "Highest Score on Super Mario Bros.," *Guinness World Records*, https://www. guinnessworldrecords.com/world-records/88009-highest-score-on-super-mario-bros#:~:- text=The%20highest%20score%20for%20a,USA)%20on%208%20January%202015.

3. "Amy Carmichael," EquipU Online Library - Kids4Truth Clubs, October 29, 2023, https://equipu.kids4truth.com/amy-carmichael/.

4. Laura Wickham, "The True Story of Betty Greene, the First Missionary Aviation Pilot," *The Good Book Blog*, September 14, 2021, https://www.thegoodbook.com/blog/ excerpts/2021/09/14/the-true-story-of-betty-greene-the-first-missionar/.

5. Carmen Hadley and David Thulin, "Wear My Crown," *Crazy for Jesus*, True Girl, 2023, mytruegirl.com.

6. "How to Be a Christian" section taken from Dannah Gresh, *Lies Girls Believe & The Truth That Sets Them Free* (Chicago: Moody Publishers, 2019), 57–59.

7. Parts of this leader's guide are adapted from Dannah Gresh, *Ruth: Becoming a Girl of Loyalty* (Chicago: Moody Publishers, 2021).

POSITIVELY JULIA!

This beautifully designed book was illustrated and designed by my friend Julia Ryan. It is her last project with me, as she is retiring to spend time with her husband, Kerry, in the beautiful mountains of Colorado. I imagine she will spend some of her time watching the wildflowers grow and tending to her vegetable garden, but I hope she jumps into her Jeep and comes to visit me in Central Pennsylvania.

We have known each other for nearly thirty years. She created the quirky brand style of True Girl, has designed nearly every book I've ever written, helped to launch a subscription box program, and has been the architect for nearly every stage set for the True Girl tour. Her artistry is unmatched.

Julia is not just a designer. She is a partner, collaborator, and visionary. She gave life to the words that I wrote and did it with great attention to detail. From studying butterflies in the Middle East to body types in ancient Persia, she was always careful to thoroughly research what she illustrated. And she did that because she loved you as much as I do. She wanted to be a part of the mission to bring you closer to your mom as you both grow closer to Jesus. And, oh, was she!

My heart is hurting as I write this. She will be so missed. But I am thankful that she is also my friend and that will never end.

What I might miss most is her emails. They never felt like work because they were full of so much joy, excitement, and friendliness. Each one was signed, "Positively, Julia." She was using the word *positively* as an adjective to describe an optimistic state of mind. But as she signs off to smell the wildflowers, I want to use the word *positively* as an adverb. Because, you see, she *Julia-fied* everything she touched with her pleasant presence. Every visual experience you have enjoyed with True Girl and Dannah Gresh has been saturated with her. It was positively Julia!

The greatest compliment to her life could be to have some of our True Girl readers become artists like Julia. To do that you not only have to keep drawing and dreaming, but also learn to love like she did. I'm praying right now that someone somewhere out there will feel this little page spark a forever life-calling to a life designed for Jesus.

Positively,

Dannah

Fill her with God's Truth so there's no room for lies.

JOIN US FOR OUR LIVE AND ON-DEMAND BIBLE STUDIES

Dig deep into God's Word with an online Bible study from True Girl!

Each study has a unique focus that will help you and the young women in your life fight the world's lies as you grow closer to Jesus. Join us for an upcoming livestream study, or access our library of recorded studies that you can view on-demand.

STUDIES YOU'LL LOVE

WITH TEACHERS YOU CAN TRUST

DANNAH GRESH   **SHANI MCKENZIE**   **JANET MYLIN**

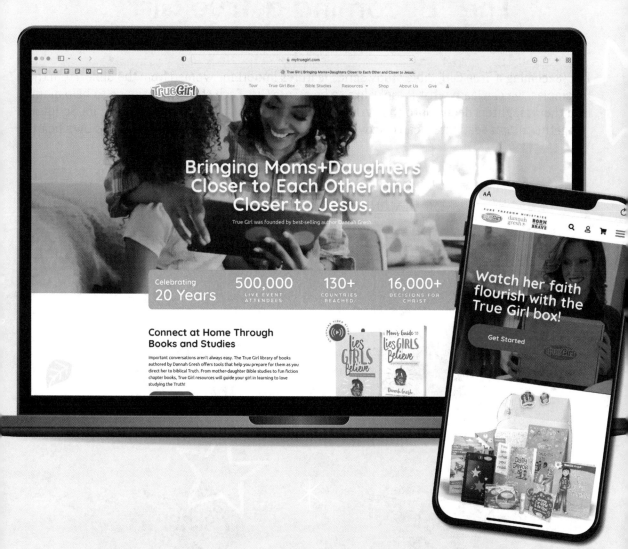

For more resources and
events for tweens, go to

MYTRUEGIRL.COM

The "Becoming a True Girl" Bible Study Series

The "Becoming a True Girl" Bible study series features important women from the Bible. From their examples, we can learn what it looks like to be a True Girl. Each study is designed to help moms lead their daughters deeply into the Word of God so they can develop a steady love for Scripture. Together, moms+daughters can discover what it means to be a True Girl after God's own heart.

MYTRUEGIRL.COM/BIBLE-STUDIES

ON-DEMAND ONLINE STUDIES AVAILABLE!

ISBN: 978-0-8024-2241-5

ISBN 978-0-8024-2222-4

ISBN 978-0-8024-2242-2

ISBN 978-0-8024-2243-9

mytruegirl.com